How to Set Your Heart on Fire

How to Set Your Heart on Fire

(and not just on Sundays)

Jeremy McQuoid

Authentic

Copyright © 2006 Jeremy McQuoid

12 11 10 09 08 07 06   7 6 5 4 3 2 1

First published 2006 by Authentic Media
9 Holdom Avenue, Bletchley, Milton Keynes, Bucks, MK1 1QR, UK
and 129 Mobilization Drive, Waynesboro, GA 30830-4575, USA
www.authenticmedia.co.uk
Authentic Media is a division of Send the Light Ltd., a company
limited by guarantee (registered charity no. 270162)

*The right of Jeremy McQuoid to be identified as the Author of
this Work has been asserted by him in accordance with the
Copyright, Designs and Patents Act 1988.*

*All rights reserved. No part of this publication may be reproduced,
stored in a retrieval system, or transmitted in any form or
by any means, electronic, mechanical, photocopying, recording or
otherwise, without the prior permission of the publisher or a licence
permitting restricted copying. In the UK such licences are issued by the
Copyright Licensing Agency.
90 Tottenham Court Road, London, W1P 9HE*

British Library Cataloguing in Publication Data

A catalogue record for this book is available from the British Library

ISBN-13 978-1-85078-666-5
ISBN-10 1-85078-666-6

Unless otherwise stated, Scripture quotations are taken from the
HOLY BIBLE, NEW INTERNATIONAL VERSION
Copyright © 1973, 1978, 1984 by the International Bible Society®.
Used by permission of Hodder & Stoughton Limited.
All rights reserved worldwide.

Cover design by jaffa:design
Print Management by Adare Carwin
Printed in Great Britain by J.H. Haynes & Co., Sparkford

Dedication

To Elizabeth

Contents

Acknowledgements	ix
Introduction	xi

Part One The Heart of the Matter

1 The Heart is the 'Centre' of Life	3

Part Two First Chamber: A Heart that Burns for God's Glory

2 God's Glory Revealed	15
3 Understanding the Glory of God	28
4 Living for the Glory of God	37

Part Three Second Chamber: A Heart that Burns for God's People

5 The Whole New Meaning of 'Love'	49
6 The Issues We Can't Avoid	60

Part Four Third Chamber: A Heart that Burns for God's World

7 The Longings of God	81
8 Reaching Out with God's Love	92
9 A Desire for All Nations	102

Part Five Fourth Chamber: A Heart that Burns for God's Return

   10 Jesus is Coming Again   115
   11 Get Ready to Meet Jesus   127

Epilogue   141

Acknowledgements

Several people have been a great help in making this book a reality. I am grateful to Keith Danby and those at Authentic Media for taking the risk with a very naïve first time author, and especially to Debbie Bunn for her careful editing of the manuscript.

The 'burning heart' is more caught that taught, and much of my desire to write comes from seeing the lives of people up close who have exemplified to me the passions described in the book. My parents John and Valerie McQuoid showed me from my earliest years what the burning heart truly is – Mum is now with the Lord, Dad continues to live for him, and to both I owe a great deal.

My in-laws David and Rosemary Vardy have, through their generosity, vision for God's work, and constant encouragement, continued to fan that flame. To be able to see God shine so clearly in both sets of parents, is a rare privilege, and I am thankful to them and to him.

I must also thank the two churches where I have been privileged to serve as pastor. Thornhill Church in Cardiff, and Deeside Christian Fellowship in Aberdeen are fine examples of congregations who 'think big' for God's Kingdom. It is an honour to be part of their vision.

And special thanks to Elizabeth, my wife. I am grateful not only for her thoughtful reading of the manuscript, and help with the study questions, but also for her patience in the long hours I am not at home, and her constant loving support as a partner in ministry and in life.

May the Lord be pleased with this book, and use it for his glory.

> For from him and through him
> and to him areall things.
> To him be glory forever! Amen. (Rom. 11:36)

Ps 139 - 23, 24

Introduction

> Were not our hearts burning within us while he talked with us ... and opened the Scriptures to us? (Lk. 24:32)

If ever there was a story to excite, if ever there was a life to live, if ever there was a cause to die for, it is the Kingdom story, the Kingdom life, the Kingdom cause.

Most Christians feel that way in principle at least. But if we are honest, the reality of Christian living and experience in the Western world in particular, is a far cry from the passion that the message of the Kingdom should ignite in our hearts. The emotions that we often express in times of praise on a Sunday are rarely translated into 'fiery' Christian living from Monday to Saturday. If we scrutinize our lives before God as the Bible encourages us to (Ps. 139:23), we should admit, as Christ followers living in an increasingly secular society, that our faith is often passion*less* and our spiritual lives are dreary and inconsistent.

True, we *think* about great things on a Sunday – a miraculous God who can do anything, whose love for us is boundless. Many of our worship songs speak quite openly about giving our all for God.

The trouble is, such wonderful sentiments seem a total contradiction to the reality of the daily grind. It is true that 'love so amazing *demands* my soul, my life, my all', but so often it does not receive that level of devotion. At the moment the World Cup is on and I have an image in my mind of thousands of English fans, their faces painted with a red cross, shouting for 11 players as though their lives depended on it. The passion etched on their faces should be the kind of passion that stirs me to Kingdom living from the moment I wake up every day. A red cross should be blazoned over my heart and I should live for the gospel of Jesus Christ as though he were returning today – because he might.

Whether we are by personality logical people or creative ones, emotional or pensive, laid-back or dynamic, the challenge is the same – we are called to live *passionate* Christian lives. A thirsty love for God in this generation should be the driving force of our lives, but we allow our passions to be quelled by the 'spirit' of this age – a 'spirit' of materialism, image and self-absorption. We have become lovers of ourselves rather than lovers of God (cf. 2 Tim. 3:1-5).

Colosseum Christians

I have recently returned from a few days spent in Rome. Standing in the middle of the huge Colosseum, my mind raced to some of the first Christians who must have stood in that intense arena.

There was no room in the Colosseum for spiritual apathy. The first martyrs had the courage of their Christian convictions. In front of 55,000 Romans baying for blood, these believers would demonstrate their passion for the Lord in the most emphatic way possible – as a later church historian would comment, 'the blood of the martyrs is the seed of the church' (Eusebius, *Church History*, vol. VIII). We tend to glorify those early Christians as 'super saints' – distant, almost unreal heroes from a legendary past. But they were ordinary men and women like you and me, living under a savage pagan state, who were simply too passionate about Jesus Christ to ever denounce him in public.

Thank God the times we live in, at least in the West, are not as dangerous for believers as Christianity's first steps in a hostile world. Yet I know that one day I will stand in front of God's throne alongside these pulsating Colosseum Christians. They had no greater supernatural power available to them than I have at my disposal today. So why is my commitment so pale in comparison? Is it simply the different context in which I have to exercise my faith? If the Lord placed a spiritual thermometer on my heart, would it register a fever or a tepid 'lukewarm' like the Christians in the church of Laodicea (Rev. 3:16)? Our Lord deserves the same passionate devotion from us his twenty-first century disciples as he received from his first century followers. A few times in zealous prayer meetings I have heard people ask God to bring persecution on the church of today so that out of suffering, when our devotion to Christ is truly placed 'on the line', a passionate faith might be stirred within us. While I appreciate their point, I would never pray such a thing. But it has been an increasing prayer in my own spiritual life that I would display to God something of the zeal of these first martyrs.

Authentic Christians

Do we have to wait for the ultimate test of martyrdom before our souls are stirred for God? Or is it possible to be *alive* to God, when the world around us is asleep? The New Testament barely recognizes 'lukewarm' Christianity. Mark tells us that believing in Jesus is like taking up a cross as a condemned man walking to his place of crucifixion (Mk. 8:34). There is no distinction in the Bible between 'believers' and 'disciples'. To believe in Christ at all means that we are willing to passionately lay down our lives for him every day.

The Gospel writers make a distinction between the 'crowds' that listened to Jesus' teaching, and the disciples who left everything to follow him. At the end of the Sermon on the Mount, the 'crowds' are 'amazed at his teaching' (Mt. 7:28), but who are the true people of the Kingdom?

The 'crowds' are those who love a good sermon, who attend all the church services, and even give some of their income to good causes. But they do not leave everything to follow him. They do not leave their fishing nets and their father standing in a boat to follow Jesus, like Peter and Andrew, James and John. They do not get up from their tax booths, never to return again, like Matthew. They are deliberately labelled 'crowds', the faceless multitude of religious people intrigued by Jesus, but definitely not 'disciples' – true learners of the Master who will carry his cross. In which camp are we?

Sadly the Christian church has often reduced commitment to Christ to a one line prayer, or a moving moment of decision in a service. I am certainly not wishing to undermine the importance of a decision for Christ, or an 'altar call'. Many of us can point to a decisive moment of decision in our Christian experience. But let us make no mistake – such a prayer is only the beginning of a life commitment according to the New Testament.

Jesus told us that the only real way to find our lives in the hereafter was to 'lose' our lives down here. Passionate Christian living is all about taking up a cross with the inscription 'condemned to die' engraved upon it. It is all about giving away our lives, surrendering our personal dreams and desires to pursue the Kingdom, so that, on the last day when the Kingdom is revealed in all its splendour, we might 'find' our lives again (Mk. 8:35).

So where does the inspiration come from to give away our lives in the context of the comfortable, materialistic, spiritually indifferent culture in which we live? Do we have to wait for persecution before passion sparks? How can our hearts rise above this climate of indifference? We will attempt to answer these questions in this book. But they are not new. In fact they were asked indirectly at the climax of Jesus' life.

Disappointed disciples

In Luke 24, we find two perplexed disciples making a weary journey from Jerusalem. These well-meaning disciples were like many Christians today – they were walking back to disappointed lives. These disciples were not the average 'pew warmers'. They had taken considerable risks to place their hope in Christ. After seeing Jesus' miracles and listening to the compelling authority of his teaching, the Emmaus disciples had left their sleepy village life with high hopes. They had met the Messiah. This Jesus was the one who would free Israel from its slavery, and usher in God's Kingdom.

Life with Christ was going to be glorious. Yet their hopes had been shattered on what must have seemed like a very bad Friday. Their grand aspirations for life with this wonderful Jesus seemed like a cruel joke now. It was time to return to the dreary reality of village life.

The Sunday/Monday turnaround

The experience of those Emmaus disciples that first Easter Sunday is so much like our Sunday/Monday turnaround. On Sunday as we join with a community of God's people to sing his praises, and are challenged by his Word, we have bright hopes – our souls are stirred. Anything seems possible. Jesus is the glorious and miraculous Son of God, reigning in heaven, poised to bring God's Kingdom to earth.

But then Monday comes. We go to work, and exactly the same Jesus seems irrelevant to everyone else. His dignified name is only mentioned in obscene throwaway lines. Clinging to the Christ of the cross seems so out of date. Often national church leaders do nothing to cure our depression. Bishops frequently appear on television reducing faith in Christ to being a good neighbour, or slipping some money into the Salvation Army box on the street corner. We have switched off the lights on Colosseum Christianity and become a charity case.

In these surroundings it is not surprising that so many Christians, like the two on the road to Emmaus, are walking back to a disappointed life. We find little to drive us in our private devotional lives. Our work is so demanding, and looking after the family so exhausting, that our Bible feels a very unattractive alternative to the TV at 10 p.m. after a hard day, and any effort at serious praying soon dissolves into slumber. Do we have to wait another six days for sunny Sundays, and the shadowy dream to burn again?

The burning heart

But that first Easter Sunday was suddenly lit up for these disappointed disciples, as a mysterious stranger joined their lonely trudge. He questioned why the disciples were so down at heart. The disciples were puzzled: 'Haven't you heard what happened to Jesus of Nazareth these past few days?'

And almost imperceptibly, as the stranger replied with an authority that was strangely familiar, disappointment and despair were transformed into passionate zeal. 'Did not the Christ have to suffer these things and then enter his glory?' And beginning with Moses and all the Prophets, he explained to them what was said in all the Scriptures concerning himself' (Lk. 24:26,27).

I wish I had been there to hear Jesus explain how he fulfilled the promises of God laid down over centuries in the Old Testament. This was no ordinary Sunday sermon. In an instant, a flame was lit within these disciples that would never be extinguished.

> *Were not our hearts burning within us* while he talked with us on the road and opened the Scriptures to us? (Lk. 24:32, my italics)

In one moment of sovereign revelation, these disciples were *caught up in the mind of God*. The Lord of glory had been speaking to them. Suddenly, they saw themselves in the sweeping plans of God.

For the first time in their lives, they were able to read God's intentions. In an instant, they were no longer lost in morose self-pity and broken dreams. They began to think the thoughts of God with him, and the world was a different place, full of possibilities.

Caught up in the mind of God

What is this 'burning heart' that lit up the disciples' lives? Was it a moment of excitement that would soon fizzle out? Or was it something more permanent, more life changing? We will address these questions in later chapters. It is my conviction that modern day disciples can know the secret of the 'burning heart' every moment of life – in fact, we *must* know it, if our lives are going to truly count for God in this generation. The burning heart begins, as it did with those first disciples, with a *change of focus*. Our minds need to shift from a self-obsessed world, to a God-shaped mindset where his eternal Kingdom fills our vision.

Why does God never cease to be passionate about his will and his world, when he sees much deeper into the spiritual lethargy of our age than we ever could? He should be more disappointed and disillusioned than we are. Why is his soul never struck with apathy? Is it not because the sovereign Lord is caught up in the glory of his own character and his own eternal plans? If we, as twenty-first century disciples, are to learn the secret of the burning heart, we need to *think God's thoughts with him*.

We need to expose ourselves to God's mind and will. We need to be caught up in the full sweep of God's glorious Kingdom plans. The cure for a parched, disappointed soul who knows that God deserves our best, is to be caught up in the mind of God. Regardless of the state of my church, or of my society, of my family, or my workplace, God's Kingdom is constantly compelling. God's mind is constantly full and satisfying. God himself is the source of the burning heart.

The passions of God

In the rest of this book we will examine the passions of God and learn how to share his thoughts with him. How can we think the thoughts of God after him? What *does* God think about? What are his priorities, his delights, his aims? What excites God?

My prayer is that this book will encourage you to look beyond the current limitations and disappointments of your life. These thoughts come to you from a heart that knows what it is like to simply go through the motions with God. If you are like me, you can become so self-critical about your lack of passion for the Kingdom of God, that you can lose all perspective on what you are truly living for. You either sink into a mire of guilt that is not God honouring, or you simply pretend that your spiritual life is healthier than it really is.

This book is not about guilt, or about pretence. It is about acknowledging honestly where we stand with God, and then looking to God for some help and direction. I am not suggesting that there is some spiritual 'magic wand' that turns every disappointing moment of life into a golden sunset. Nor am I wishing to undermine a deep experience of God you may have had in the past – such times can be precious and life changing. But we can run out of steam so quickly, and lose our focus on what really matters.

My aim is to help focus our lives on the plans and passions of God. Surely that is in line with the work of the

Holy Spirit in our hearts? All spiritual disillusionment ultimately boils down to losing sight of the splendour of God. If we get caught up in something of his glory, if our hearts can learn how to burn again like those simple Emmaus disciples, then there will be no room or time for disappointment. The Kingdom will be too urgent, and the King too compelling.

Review

- It is possible to have a burning heart, even in the middle of a dying church and a post-Christian nation. Our hearts are set ablaze when we lose ourselves in the passions of God.
- If our hearts start to think God's thoughts with him, we will experience that same soul illuminating excitement that led disappointed disciples from Emmaus to scurry back on a dark and dangerous road to the upper room they had left behind.

For personal study

- In what ways has the spirit of this age 'a spirit of materialism, image and self-absorption' seeped into the church and compromised its passion for God?
- If God put a spiritual thermometer on your heart, how would it read?
- What criteria do you use to gauge your spiritual temperature and passion for Christ?
- The author writes that 'all spiritual disillusionment ultimately boils down to losing sight of the splendour of God'. What is there in your life that causes you to lose sight of God's glory?

Part One:
The Heart of the Matter

1

The Heart is the 'Centre' of Life

> Above all else, guard your heart, for it is the wellspring of life (Prov. 4:23).

All spiritual excitement and disillusionment ultimately boils down to the health, or otherwise, of our hearts. My wife and I have recently had our second child. It was a truly thrilling moment when we went for a scan to see our baby on a computer screen for the first time. The midwife who was conducting the scan seemed to know instinctively where all the body parts were, while the picture on the screen in front of my untrained eye just looked like a blob.

What struck us most powerfully, as we saw this little life taking shape, was the crucial role of the heart. Yes, we were interested to see the head and hands and toes, but the nurse was especially drawn to the heart. There is no clearer sign of life and vitality than a beating heart. All of life in the body seems to flow out of the heart.

It was an unforgettable moment for us to finally see our baby's heartbeat. Our child was alive. But the nurse wanted to get a better look. The heart was too critical an organ to be satisfied with a simple heartbeat. Elizabeth had to turn over on her side so that the monitor could capture a cross-section of the heart. And then I discovered what the midwife was looking for.

You could see quite clearly on the monitor the *four chambers of the heart*. Each chamber of this tiny organ was so vital to the whole, and the heart was so crucial to life and vitality in the body. Little wonder the nurse spent so much time examining the heart of our tiny baby to see if all was well.

Understanding how our hearts work

The heart is just as vital in spiritual life as it is in physical life. If we are ever to discover the secret of the burning heart, we need to understand how our hearts work in spiritual terms. Just as all of our physical life seems to flow out of our physical hearts, so all our spiritual life flows out of our spiritual hearts; just as our hearts pump blood to all parts of our body to keep us physically alive, so in the spiritual world our hearts provide the motivation and the energy to keep our souls alive to God and his passions. Heart trouble is just as serious in the spiritual world as it is in the physical.

We most often link the heart with our emotions – when a boy meets the girl of his dreams on a romantic encounter, his heart beats faster. The heart is the symbol of St Valentine's Day, and provides the lyrics for most of our pop songs. As a result we often misunderstand what the Bible is saying when it talks about our hearts in spiritual terms. The Hebrew idea of 'heart' is much fuller than our modern concept of pure emotions.

The Heart is the 'Centre' of Life

The word for 'heart' in Hebrew originally meant 'centre'. The heart in Bible terms is the very 'centre' of our beings. Our heart is the place where our character is formed. This, of course, involves our emotions because God made us to be emotional beings, but it is so much more than that. The heart is the seat of our wills, the source of our passions. Your heart is quite simply who you are as a person. It's what makes you tick.

The book of Proverbs provides us with a beautiful picture of our hearts as the 'wellspring of life' (Prov. 4:23). Just as our arteries move oxygen-filled blood to every part of the body, so our hearts in a spiritual sense are like a fountain, constantly pumping our desires and ideas, our emotions and plans around our beings, to motivate and dictate our whole lives. Jesus himself said

> The good man brings good things out of the good stored up in his heart (Lk. 6:45).

Every word that comes from our mouths is the result of the ideas and passions we have stored up in our hearts

> For out of the overflow of his heart his mouth speaks (Lk. 6:45).

The fuller meaning of heart in the Bible sense is very clear in Jesus' teaching. Jesus said to his disciples, 'out of the heart come evil thoughts, murder, adultery, sexual immorality, theft, false testimony, slander' (Mt. 15:19).

This is a negative example which demonstrates that 'heart' in the Bible is much more than pure emotion. Here, what our heart does is connected with our 'thoughts' – we think with our heart. What goes on in our heart produces our actions – 'murder, adultery ... theft' and so on – we act with our heart. The inner process of our hearts is the lamp that lights up our whole being, either positively or negatively.

Little wonder that Proverbs implores us, 'Above all else...' above every other consideration in life, '... *guard* your heart' (Prov. 4:23, my italics) – guard your inner life of thoughts, will, emotions, and desires. Your heart is who you are! You cannot act, think or speak in a different way to your heart's impulses. To put it another way, the quality of my discipleship is decided in my heart long before I ever act on these inner impulses. How important it is then to place 'quality controls' on what I allow to influence my heart.

Guarding your heart

The burning heart begins with guarding our hearts, as Proverbs implores us, but this is no passive action. We might think of a 'guard' as the motionless servant of the Queen who hangs around endlessly at the doors of Buckingham Palace, keeping her Majesty from harm. There are many well-meaning Christians who feel that in order to keep their hearts pure for God, they need to be equally passive – they need to separate themselves off from the world like hermits so that they ensure that no evil thing ever touches their beings. Their lives are dictated by what they *should not do* in case they offend a holy God, rather than positively giving themselves to the ambitions of God.

A burning heart is not set alight by a hermit's existence. We do not guard our hearts by refusing to mix with the 'tax collectors and sinners' of our day. Our Saviour's life was powerfully active, exhausting, and sometimes scandalous – that is why men had him hung on a cross. He was not just another harmless hermit.

Our hearts will not burn simply by doing everything we can to avoid sin. <u>Guarding our hearts means keeping our hearts healthy for God.</u> To avoid heart trouble in my body, I don't just stop eating fatty foods, I start eating a balanced diet. I positively feed my heart with nutritious energy-giving food. I take regular exercise to keep my heart strong. In the same way, my heart will not burn simply by staying away from everything wicked. I must actively pursue godly living in a fallen world.

Guarding my heart does not simply mean reading 2,000 pages of a Bible doctrine book under my duvet at night (though, that's not a bad idea). It means living out my Bible doctrine by showing kindness to my rather annoying brother who always sings too loudly in church, or the single mum who lives next door. A burning heart is an active heart. It is out on the streets and in public. It makes people stop and look and listen, and see God standing in front of them.

The burning hearts of the first Christians did not stay in the upper room, constantly studying how Christ fulfilled the Old Testament Scriptures. They spread the gospel to Jerusalem, Judea, Samaria and to the ends of the earth. They preached in the open air, in the public squares, they hired lecture halls, they spoke to people sitting on river banks, they caused riots in cities, earthquakes in prisons, upset local government officials and healed beggars. They were 'dangerous' Christians, taking the word of Christ where Satan did not want it to go.

Loving God with all our heart

My heart then is the 'centre' of my being, the central control system from which my whole life flows. The Bible calls me to guard my heart, not just by staying away from sin, but by positively pursuing righteousness in my daily life in the world. But if we understand what our hearts are, how does this help us obey the Bible's number one command?

Do you love God with all your heart? That is probably the biggest question a Christian can ask. But many of us are confused about what we're being asked. Remember that intimate moment that Jesus had with Peter, perhaps his closest friend and confidant, as they were walking along a beach shortly before Jesus was to ascend into heaven. Here was Jesus talking to the man who would carry the hopes of the fledgling church in his hands – Peter the hot-headed, big-hearted fisherman from Capernaum.

This is a moment of high tension in John's Gospel, occurring so shortly after Peter's denials and the rooster crowing. This is Jesus 'interviewing' the church's first pastor – 'Feed my sheep' (Jn. 21:17) is the clear pastoral role that Jesus gives to Peter. So what is the burning question that Jesus wants to ask the church's most important recruit?

It is the question of all questions

Simon, son of John, do you love me? (Jn. 21:16)

Jesus is not primarily concerned in this interview to talk about Peter's strategy for taking the gospel into Asia and Europe. He is not intent on teaching Peter, in this moment of moments, the mode of baptism he should favour, or giving guidelines about which new apostle Peter should appoint following Judas' defection. Jesus is interested in Peter's heart. Jesus wants to know if Peter's heart is ready to burn for his Master – 'Peter, do you love me?'

The Heart is the 'Centre' of Life

What is Jesus asking? Is he asking, 'Peter, how do you feel about me?' I'm sure that was partly in Jesus' mind, but it is much more than that. Yes, this was a question of the heart, but the heart is much bigger than emotions. We have confused loving God with the fuzzy emotions we experience during a moving song in a church service. I can feel great about God in any given moment, but still not have a burning heart. In fact if I regularly have strongly fluctuating emotions as a Christian – 'in the clouds' when the songs are being sung, but switched off when the Bible is being preached – then that is a good sign that I don't have the burning heart the Bible talks about.

Jesus challenges Peter to show his love for him, not simply with the emotional response of a few words – Peter was good at that (cf. Jn. 13:37) – but with the whole of his life. 'Peter, will you feed my sheep? Will you make it the goal of your life to take care of my church? Will you watch over wandering disciples, will you teach them with patience and gentle instruction, will you have sleepless nights worrying about fellow disciples – will you feed my sheep?'

Driven by the call of God

Loving God with all his heart meant for Peter being totally driven by the call of God on his life. 'Do you love me?' was a question with barbed wire on it. Loving Jesus with all his heart would ultimately mean for Peter being 'lead . . . where you do not want to go'. Loving God with all his heart would mean a cross for Peter, allowing someone else to 'stretch out your hands' (Jn. 21:18). Loving God with all his heart meant surrendering his mind and will and soul and strength to God, laying down his life for the sake of the Kingdom.

A burning heart is not the passing emotion of a moment – it is a whole life given to God. It is a will shaped by God, a mind captivated by God, a body broken for God. My heart is the 'centre' of my being, it is what makes me tick. My whole spiritual life flows from my heart. C. Ryder Smith, in his book *The Bible Doctrine of Man* (Peterborough: Epworth Press, 1951), sums up the full implications of the word 'heart' in the Bible, when he gives his own translation of the Great Commandment

> You shall love the Lord your God with all your heart – *that is* with all your soul, mind and strength.

Our heart includes our soul, our mind and our strength. A burning heart feels passionately for God, thinks deeply about God, and works tirelessly with God. I cannot say 'I love God' until God and his Kingdom dominate my thinking, my doing and my wanting, just as much as they affect my feelings.

The chambers of the heart

If I recognize that my heart really also means my will, my thoughts, my passions and my energy, then I need to know what to give my heart to. What should I want? What should I be thinking? What should I be feeling? What should I be doing? We mentioned in the Introduction that a burning heart is caught up in the passions of God. What are those passions that should drive us? What are the sweeping plans of God that will make my mind, my will, my thoughts and my strength truly burn for him?

The analogy of the four chambers of the heart can help us to picture the four principal passions that God wants us to think about, to yearn for, to strive for, to hope in. It is my conviction that if we give our soul, mind and strength to these four passions of God, we will have a burning heart, no matter what frustrating circumstances we have to deal with in our lives. In the following chapters of this book, we will look in turn at each of the four chambers of a heart that truly burns for God.

In chamber one, God wants our hearts to burn for his glory. We will discover that the glory of God is what ultimately drives God to do everything that he ever does. So if our hearts are to burn like the Emmaus disciples, we need to think about, feel passionately about, yearn and strive for the glory of God in this world.

In chamber two, God wants our hearts to burn for his people. God loves all nations, but he especially loves those who belong to him. He calls us his children, his very own. The church is the bride of Christ, the apple of God's eye, and God is longing to spend eternity with his chosen people. So if our hearts are to burn like inspired disciples on the Emmaus Road, we need to think, feel and act towards God's people with all the longing and intensity that he does.

In chamber three, God wants our hearts to burn for his world. God loved the world so much that he sacrificed his one and only son to save it. That world includes those countless millions who have rejected his offer of salvation up to this point. That world includes nations across the globe 'from every tribe and tongue and people and language'. If our hearts are to beat in tune with God, we need to be Christians who look beyond our own concerns, and the concerns of our church, to long for a world that may never experience the passion God has for it.

In chamber four of our hearts, God wants us to burn for his return. The earliest Christians whose burning hearts blazed a trail for the gospel through Asia and Europe within a single generation – those believers used to close their church services with the one word prayer, *'maranatha!'* – come quickly, Lord. If our hearts are to burn like the church in the days of the apostles, we need to stop feeling so at home in this world, and start to long for the coming again of our Lord Jesus Christ, with holy, urgent living.

Review

- Our hearts are the central control system of our spiritual life. We think with our hearts, act with our hearts, will with our hearts, as well as feel with them.
- God wants us to think his thoughts with him, to act in line with his Kingdom, bend our wills to his holy desires, and feel his passions!
- The four chambers of the heart provide a helpful illustration, as we understand the four primary passions of God that should dominate our thinking, willing, acting, and feeling.

For personal study

- In what practical ways can we 'guard our hearts'?
- Why do you think Jesus asked Peter the question 'Do you love me?' What kind of evidence do you think Jesus is looking for before we can say that we truly love him?
- Why is it important to be aware of the passions of God? What difference do you think it would make to your life if you discovered God's chief passions?

Part Two:
First Chamber: A Heart that Burns for God's Glory

2

God's Glory Revealed

> . . . to him be glory in the church and in Christ Jesus throughout all generations, for ever and ever! Amen. (Eph.3:21)

Nothing sets a Christian's heart ablaze quite like the glory of God. There is a desire within us as human beings which searches for something greater than ourselves. All peoples everywhere have a natural instinct to worship, to praise, to stand in awe, whether they are desert nomads bowing down to a mountain, or astronomers lost in the wonder of the vast reaches of outer space. We are captivated by majesty. That should not surprise us. We were made that way by the Majestic One.

Our sense of awe and wonder, our desire to worship, turns us instinctively into spiritual detectives, searching for something that can satisfy our longing for transcendence. The French mathematician and devoted Christian, Blaise Pascal, famously referred to this worship desire as a 'God shaped gap' in our lives. The missing dimension in our souls that will leave us empty until we find something 'ultimate' enough to fill it, is the glory of God. God's glory does not disappoint us.

The glory of God refers to the way God has revealed himself to us. God's glory is the full shining out of his character. The way in which God has revealed himself through creation, and most especially in his written revelation, the Bible, is full of mystery, power and wonder. In the writings of Scripture, God woos us with his unfailing love, but distances us with his absolute holiness. He soothes our hearts with his mercy and grace, but wounds and frightens us with his wrath. He compares himself to a 'mother' and a 'judge', a 'father' and a 'fire', a 'friend', and an 'enemy'.

He tenderly carries his lambs in his arms, but will ferociously judge the wicked in an end-of-time 'blood bath'. Jesus Christ is referred to as 'the radiance of God's glory' (Heb. 1:3), and he fully displays God's character in all its glory. At the Last Supper, the disciple John rests in perfect comfort and security on the chest of Jesus his friend (Jn. 13:25). But when John sees a vision of Jesus in his resurrected glory, he falls at his feet 'as though dead' (Rev. 1:17).

This is the enigma, the fascination, the limitless mystery of the glory of God. He has revealed himself as the ultimate sovereign Lord of the universe who controls and sustains all things, and yet he calls me his friend, his brother. I am a precious child of the King of kings.

A kaleidoscope of glory

God's glory is like a kaleidoscope, full of many colours, appreciable in different ways from different angles. Wherever you look there is beauty and consistency. He is

God's Glory Revealed

not many gods, but one infinite, timeless, sovereign, holy, all knowing, all powerful, all wise and wonderful God. But he allows himself to be known by us. He allows us to experience him in all his delight and danger, tenderness and terror.

<u>To know this God is to find the greatest treasure in the universe.</u>

> Let not the wise man boast of his wisdom or the strong man boast of his strength or the rich man boast of his riches, but let him who boasts boast about this: that he understands and knows me (Jer. 9:23,24).

If we truly knew God in all his glory, our minds would be captivated and satisfied, our souls would be full and rich and our hearts would burn forever.

A life pursuit

However, knowing God in all his glory is not automatic. <u>Knowing God is the project of a lifetime.</u> It is the great pursuit of life. The ultimate goal of all our lives, according to the book of Revelation, is for God to live among his people, and for us to experience his glory 'up close and personal', without any hindrance. This is the 'big picture' of redemption, the goal of all God's plans from Eden to the 'new heavens and the new earth'. God wants us to share in his glory.

At the end of Revelation, at the culmination of all things, the voice from heaven shouts out

> Now the dwelling of God is with men, and he will live with them. They will be his people, and God himself will be with them and be their God (Rev. 21:3).

The picture portrayed is not of sitting having a chat with God as we play our harps and find a comfortable cloud for all eternity. Eternity will be consumed with the worship of God! We will fully discover the reason we were made – to enjoy God in all his endless beauty, and live for his pleasure.

If we are to fulfil this purpose, the pursuit of God's glory should engross us and be reflected in our everyday lives. But the reason why so many Christians are struggling to be passionate about their faith is because their understanding of God's glory is far too small. Our hearts can only burn when we begin to understand the complete panorama of God's glory, the 'big picture'.

Editing God

The moment we start to limit God, or make him into someone less than he really is, we lose something of his glory. When we begin to overemphasize one facet of his character at the expense of another, the kaleidoscope becomes dull, and we quench the fire in our burning hearts. More seriously, if we have built an image of God in our minds which is not accurate, because it is incomplete, we become idol worshippers. We are not worshipping the true God of heaven, but a god of our own making, who pleases us. This is precisely what God warned his people Israel away from when he first revealed himself to them on top of Mount Sinai.

He commanded

God's Glory Revealed

> You shall not make for yourself an idol in the form of anything in heaven above or on the earth beneath or in the waters below. You shall not bow down to them or worship them (Ex. 20:4,5).

God didn't give this command simply because he was concerned about Israel worshipping the gods of the nations around about her. He was also concerned about his people wanting to turn him into an idol. For example, God would be angry if the Israelites carved an image of an eagle to represent God's wisdom, and brought that carving home and worshipped that instead of the living and true God. Israel would then be limiting God in some way. They would overemphasize the fact that God was wise, but might diminish his holiness or his mercy, his justice or his grace.

Not only so, but carved images were very 'user-friendly'. They were portable and could be carried around wherever the worshipper went. God did not want his people to think of him as 'user-friendly.' <u>He is awesome.</u> Even the heavens cannot contain him. Either God's people accepted and worshipped him for who he truly was, in all his awesome power and splendour, or they were not worshipping him at all. Worshipping a part of God was idol worship in God's eyes.

Christians today have not obeyed this most fundamental of commands. We have 'edited' God in many different, equally damaging ways. Often with the best of motives, we have carved out a god who is a pale reflection of the Lord Almighty.

'austere' god

Some sincere Christians will overemphasize God's holiness, his distance, his 'unapproachability'. He is a God of terror and smoke and fire. He is a God to be spoken to only in ornate and beautified language. We must speak to him at a distance, not as an intimate friend, or a caring father – that would be to belittle his solemn honour. We cannot tell him how we really feel, or share our real frustrations and disappointments with him. We are nothing more than worms in his sight. We dare not question his ways. He is only to be worshipped in the most reverential quietness and contemplation.

There is, of course, a great deal of truth in this understanding of God. God is holy, awesome and fearful. We cannot approach him any old way we like. We need to fully appreciate the ways God is not like us, his 'otherness.' But, an overemphasis on God's 'unapproachability' leaves many Christians feeling joyless, and insecure. They are not excited about the sheer thrill of knowing God. They mourn for their sin, and become so deeply aware of their failures, that they fail to see the plan God has for their lives.

It is true that confessing our sins is crucial for a daily relationship with a holy God (1 Jn. 1:9), but being constantly weighed down with our lack of holiness hardly does justice to what God has done for us through the cross of Jesus. Jesus died to *take away* our sin. We can enjoy the absolute freedom of forgiveness (Rom. 8:1). God is not glorified when our lives are so hindered and weighed down by our own unworthiness, it becomes like a chain around our necks. The result of God saving us, is that we are God's 'work of art' (Eph. 2:10). We have been recreated in Christ to do good works. We represent God as his 'ambassadors'. We begin to recover our true humanity in Christ, a humanity which was 'very good' when God first made us in his own image.

We are not doing justice to the glory of God when we walk around with solemn faces simply because we want to defend God's holiness with complete reverence. God wants us to delight in him.

> I will go to the altar of God, to God, my joy and my delight. I will praise you with the harp, O God, my God (Ps. 43:4).

The Psalms pulsate with pleasure in God – the incredible truth that the holy God of heaven is *'my* God'. Our hearts miss out on the burning pleasure they were created for, when we *only* think of God as unapproachable.

The deep things of God are not necessarily the sombre things of God. Sombre Christians sometimes feel as though they are the last remaining true worshippers, fighting against the shallowness of other Christian belief. But a god who is *only* unapproachable, and *only* holy, is a shallow god. He is an idol. Our hearts cannot burn when we are worshipping an idol – a false god who I know and revere only as the holy judge, and not *my loving father*. It is so easy to lose the full kaleidoscope of God's glory, and the results are catastrophic for our souls. Our hearts dry up like a leaf in winter.

God wants our lives under his rule to be overflowing with joy. Jesus intended us to drink so deeply of the Holy Spirit within us, that 'streams of living water' (Jn. 7:38) would flow from us to the world around us. There is no contradiction between holiness and joy, reverence and spontaneity in worship. In fact to emphasize one without the other is to limit God's glory and be left with half a god and half a heart!

The 'inoffensive' god

The church of the 'austere' god is in decline today. Many Christians have understandably rebelled against what they see as the repressive, dour view of God they have grown up with. Sadly, many of these Christians often end up being guilty of a similar crime to their predecessors. They want to remove forever the solemn image of a God of 'fire and smoke' from their minds, so they over-emphasize the 'positive' aspects of God's character. Knowing God to them is almost exclusively about love, joy and peace. This is a god who offers us free forgiveness without daring to ask what our sins have been, in case that upsets us.

He is an inoffensive god, gently asking us to accept the warm breeze of his soothing love in our hearts. He wants to wrap his loving arms around us, tell us everything is 'OK', and whisper peace into our souls. He is undemanding. He understands our frailties and failures, and will continue to love and cherish us, no matter what we do or how we treat him. Again much of this caricature displays real truths about God that we don't want to downplay. There is a loving tenderness about God that is like a mother hen gathering her chicks under her wings (Mt. 23:37). I am delighted and deeply thankful that God is 'gracious and compassionate . . . slow to anger and abounding in love' (Jon. 4:2). But it is impossible to have a rich understanding of God's glory, and come to the conclusion that he is inoffensive.

Christians who only concentrate on God's 'niceness' have tremendous trouble with a God who invents hell. Whether we like it or not, hell is the direct consequence of the glory of God. His justice and wrath, his holiness and fury demand a place of eternal punishment. God loves deeply, and is full of grace, but he is not a 'soft touch', and he is certainly not inoffensive.

The picture of Jesus gently blessing children as he took them on his knee is lovely and true, but it must be balanced in our minds with the chilling picture of the warrior Jesus in Revelation. His robe is dipped in blood (Rev. 19:13), because he has returned from wiping out the enemies of God, while the angels sing his praises for unleashing God's righteous vengeance on the earth.

> He treads the winepress of the fury of the wrath of God Almighty (Rev. 19:15).

Words like 'vengeance' and 'wrath' may not be pleasant for us to think about, but it is ultimately the beauty and perfection of God's character that makes them necessary. God is angry at the wicked because their evil schemes and open defiance of his laws are an affront to his righteousness and justice. Hell and judgement are absolutely necessary if God is going to uphold the perfection of his character, and punish what is evil.

It is God's wrath against the sins of the world he created, that eventually led to the cross. The cross is the ultimate statement of God's glory. The broken, naked man hanging his head in shame reveals God's anger at our sin, the offence of our sin to the holiness of God. Yet, at the same time, it also shows us the powerful love and grace of a father weeping for his bruised son, so that he might bring many rebellious sons and daughters to heaven, to share in his glory forever.

The cross reflects the kaleidoscope of God's glory. The God of the cross is neither 'nice' nor 'inoffensive' – he is no 'soft touch'. He is altogether more magnificent and exciting than that. He is furious wrath, white-hot holiness, unsullied righteousness, lavish love, fathomless mercy, and a fountain of grace all at the same time. To reduce him to a harmless, 'inoffensive god', is to rob ourselves of the glory that sets our hearts ablaze.

The 'packaged' god

Perhaps the greatest challenge to the church in the twenty-first century, is to know how to communicate the God of the Bible in a relevant way to an increasingly unchurched, biblically illiterate society. As a pastor who preaches frequently, I am faced with this problem every week.

My fear is that many churches, who want to communicate about God in the language of today's generation (a vital principle), are actually robbing God of his glory by reducing their teaching about God to attractive 'sound bites'. The problem here is not so much an overemphasis on any one particular character trait of God. Instead it is the fact that God is being presented in a 'dumbed down' version to match the general dumbing down of communication in society.

The glory of God cannot be communicated purely through 'sound bites'. Television with its 'quick-fire', entertainment orientated approach may be the most popular and effective form of mass communication, but whether it is the most powerful vehicle to communicate the riches of the glory of God must be open to question.

There are an increasing number of visionary churches who want to present God in a TV style – slick, punchy presentations of what they perceive are the essentials of the gospel. The argument goes that TV is the way the vast majority of people receive their information in daily life.

God's Glory Revealed

So if we are to speak the peoples' language, we need to use TV-speak.

But there is a real danger inherent in an *over reliance* on this approach – a danger that I believe in years to come will lead to spiritual dwarves rather than burning-heart giants in our churches. My fear is that the kaleidoscope of God's glory, so essential to the forming of burning heart disciples, will be lost. We will become so at home with the ease and entertainment of TV church, that <u>we will lose</u> our hunger to know the Lord in all his excellence.

God has chosen to communicate to this world primarily, though not exclusively, through a 66-volume library of books, written by people from various backgrounds over thousands of years. His book is neither simple nor simplistic – it is not even instantly accessible. We must seek to make its rich message as accessible as possible to this generation, avoiding religious jargon that no outsider can relate to. But a properly rich understanding of the God of the Bible does not sit easily with sound bite church presentations.

While the absolute essentials of the gospel can be summed up in a few carefully chosen phrases, it is not a quick-fire repetition of gospel essentials that creates burning-heart Christians. Indeed even gospel essentials such as a true understanding of sin, the cross, repentance, the resurrection and the final judgement, are often sidelined in TV church.

Christians and non-Christians alike, at all stages of their faith journey, need to be confronted with the glory of God, as the Bible is taught systematically, with passionate, clear application by gifted teachers of the Word. There are no short cuts here. There never have been. As P.T. Forsyth (*Positive Preaching and the Modern Man*, Grand Rapids: Baker, 1980) said so controversially with its preaching Christianity stands or falls.

It would be a terrible tragedy to sacrifice a rich presentation of the glory of God on the altar of 'user-friendly' preaching. We must strive to find the balance between preaching that connects with the lives of twenty-first century listeners, using jargon free up-to-date language, and preaching that displays the rich tapestry of

> the glorious gospel of the blessed God, which he entrusted to me (1 Tim. 1:11).

It amazes me as I read New Testament books like Galatians, Colossians and Thessalonians, undoubtedly written to Gentile Christians in a more illiterate society, who were new to the faith, that Paul does not shy away from deep truths. He does not 'package' God to make him more accessible to these young Christians.

Quite the opposite. His aim seems to be to thrill these young believers with the glory of God. In Philippians he talks quite freely about

> the surpassing greatness of knowing Christ Jesus my Lord . . . I want to know Christ and the power of his resurrection and the fellowship of sharing in his sufferings, becoming like him in his death, and so, somehow, to attain the resurrection from the dead (Phil. 3:8,10,11).

These are not simple concepts that can be portrayed through sound bites. They are truths that need to be thought through, reached for, experienced in our souls. The passion for fiery Christian living is stirred by a deep understanding of who God is.

That is not to suggest that 'seeker-friendly' events have no place in the church. Many have been challenged in their thinking to pursue God through multimedia events that highlight the truths of Scripture in an up-to-date style. But these events should not overshadow or replace good, Bible-based teaching that presents God in all his glory. When such events simply 'dumb down' the public presentation of God for the sake of making him accessible to people, we run the risk of inviting our generation to bow down to an idol – a god who is a pale reflection of the Majestic One.

3

Understanding the Glory of God

You might be saying to yourself right now, 'I recognize the problem that comes when I edit God. I see that my passion for God can be quenched by having a limited view of his glory. But what can I do in my day-to-day life to develop a fuller, more biblically faithful view of God?'

The glory of God in Scripture

I think this begins with how we read the Bible in our own personal quiet times. If God has chosen to reveal the fullness of his character in the pages of Scripture, then we have to ask ourselves, 'Am I biased towards certain passages of Scripture and not others? Do I deliberately and repeatedly head towards those passages of Scripture which simply back up the views about God I already hold dear?'

Personally speaking, I love the book of Luke. I love the emphasis in Luke of Jesus reaching out to Gentiles and the marginalized. I love how Jesus breaks the taboos of his society to speak to women in Luke. I love the

Understanding the Glory of God

delightful insights on the work of the Holy Spirit, which we find more in Luke than any other Gospel. I love the passions behind the parable of the Prodigal Son in Luke 15. I love the theme sentence of Luke when Jesus declares that he has come to 'seek and to save those who are lost' (Lk. 19:10) following the heart-warming story of Zacchaeus, the chief tax collector who climbed the sycamore tree. I find Luke to be the best book for communicating the gospel to ordinary people today. I even love the careful, systematic way Luke writes. Perhaps because Luke was a Gentile and not a Jew, he speaks more clearly to my Western mindset. His writing resonates with my soul, and satisfies my mind.

On the other hand I confess I struggle with the Old Testament prophets. Sections of Isaiah, and particularly Jeremiah and Ezekiel I do not find pleasant reading. The oracles of the prophets seem sometimes to be disjointed and chaotic (especially in Jeremiah). Unlike the Gospel of Luke, I can't follow an easy-to-read storyline in the prophets. And when it comes to the series of 'woe' oracles against surrounding nations that these prophets utter, I find I have to plough through them, rather than relish them.

I mention those three prophets because I have read through them recently. I went to them with the mindset 'I've got to tackle these books at some time, so why not now!' Looking back on that experience, there were several days when I felt like I was just ploughing through lengthy passages that often left me puzzled. But I can honestly say I have a richer understanding of the glory of God as a result.

In actual fact, Isaiah has more to say about the glory of God than any other book. You get a more panoramic picture of God's supreme control over creation, his desire to reach the nations, and the eternal Kingdom we are heading towards as Christians from Isaiah than any other book in the Bible. I still find Luke more 'enjoyable' to read than Isaiah. It confirms again and again the truths I hold most dear about Christ. But Luke doesn't teach me about God's glory in quite the same way Isaiah does.

Jeremiah and Ezekiel, with their strange visions, are not easy going either. But I found I could relate to Jeremiah's struggles representing a God who no one else believed in – the crisis of preaching judgement from God when everyone wants you to preach soothing words. This taught me something about God as an uncompromising judge, and what it means to serve him, in a way that no other book could.

I struggled with Ezekiel's vision of living creatures and wings with eyes and wheels going to and fro (and that was only chapter 1!). I don't have those kind of complications to deal with in Luke. And yet there was something about that vision of an all seeing God, his radiance being like a rainbow, the fire, the brilliant light of his appearance, and all the connections with similar visions of God in the book of Revelation, which captivated my soul. I saw how big God is, how vast his knowledge, how beautiful his countenance, how blazing and wonderful his holiness. And I saw all that in Ezekiel, not in my favourite book, Luke.

I could never see those things from Luke. If I kept on reading only Luke, I would end up believing in a lovely Jesus who seeks the prodigals, honours women and prays in the Holy Spirit, all of which is true and biblical. But when I realize that that same Jesus is the God who owns the heavens, and wants to reach the nations as Isaiah tells me, he's the same Jesus who had to preach unpopular words of judgement just like Jeremiah did he's the same Jesus who is brilliant in his glory, has an all seeing eye, and is like fire in his holiness, *then* I begin to discover something of the kaleidoscope of God's glory.

My reading of Luke is enriched – Luke becomes even more luminous and exciting. My interest levels in Isaiah, Jeremiah and Ezekiel increase because though I have not understood everything, I have glimpsed something of their amazing messages. But most of all, God has grown in my heart. I have got rid of my 'safe' god who always looks the same every time I come to him, and I am uncovering little by little the God of burning glory who can satisfy my heart and soul and mind forever. He has become to me the God of the prodigal, the God of the universe and the God who inspires my preaching and serving all at the same time. And as the Spirit constantly feeds me in my appreciation of this limitless God as I learn to read widely in Scripture, it changes my prayer life, increases my faith, and most of all, gives me a fuller heart for worship.

Being disciplined and learning to read a balanced diet from all portions of the Scripture – the tough as well as the tender, the easy to follow as well as the 'plough through' passages – is a day-to-day practical way we can increase our love for the glory of God in all its vastness. Ultimately reading widely in Scripture is a labour of love, as we work hard to appreciate all the ways God has chosen to reveal his glory.

The glory of God in my prayer life

Together with a broader range of Bible reading, we can develop a deeper appreciation of God's glory through our prayer lives. It is a very good practice at the end of a reading to pray back to God some of the thoughts of his character that you have just read in the passage. It helps you focus on what God has been teaching you in your reading.

It's so easy to slip into a dull routine in a quiet time. We have some vague reading in the Psalms for example (just because the Bible happened to open there), tick that off our 'to do' list, and then base our prayer time almost exclusively around our shopping list of personal requests for God. The pastor and author Stuart Briscoe tells the story of a little boy who was getting ready to say his prayers one night. Before he climbed the stairs to his bedroom, he went into the lounge and said to his parents: 'Does anybody want anything?'

It is very tempting to close our Bibles and get straight into our shopping list, 'Father, will you do this for me . . .?' If you are tempted to do that, just stop next time and say, 'What has God just taught me about himself in this passage?' Spend a minute in quiet. Empty your mind of everything else that seems urgent in your day to bring to God. Ask God's Spirit to teach you more about who God is. To make what you have been reading real to your soul.

Begin your prayers with worship. Teach yourself to adore God for who he is, not just ask him for what you want. You can guarantee that the Spirit will help you if you have a serious desire to worship God in your prayers. Be still. Give God time to speak to you about his glory. Even if you have only ten minutes to pray in the morning, spend five of those minutes in worship. You'll find after a while that even those urgent requests begin to feel a little less urgent in your soul. God becomes your focus. He knows what you need before you ask him anyway. Why not spend more time appreciating him, before you ask him for anything?

Understanding the Glory of God

In our rushed lives today it is not easy to cultivate this worshipful prayer life. From my own experience, this approach does not make every quiet time a taste of heaven. It takes time, and a quiet room in the house. The phone can still ring at the wrong time. My soul can be just so troubled about the day that worship gets lost in the anxiety. God understands these things. But we are much more likely to adore God over a period of time if we are intentional about it. How much do we really *want* to appreciate him? Those who wrote the Westminster Catechism were right when they said

> the chief end of man is to glorify God and enjoy him forever.

How much time do we really spend learning how to enjoy God? Perhaps it takes getting up 15 minutes earlier than usual. Perhaps using a pen and notepad would help, and making bullet points about what the passage teaches me about God's glory. But O, how our hearts might start to burn if we looked at our prayer times as an opportunity to explore and discover and enjoy God. His Spirit will meet any effort you make in this, with grace and fresh insights. Knowing God is not about your intellectual prowess, but about the thirst in your soul to discover him. Don't quench that thirst with humdrum, predictable prayers. If you thirst for God in your prayers as much as your Bible reading, your spiritual life will depend less on how well the preacher managed to preach on Sunday, and more on your own personal communion with God.

The glory of God in song

Christian music is also a way we can grow in our appreciation of the full scope of God's glory. What a great way to learn about the glory of God and respond in worship as you

> sing psalms, hymns and spiritual songs with gratitude in your hearts to God (Col. 3:16).

Every time we talk about songs and hymns we inevitably enter the debate of traditional versus contemporary worship.

Without wishing to enter an age-old debate I am unlikely to win, let's remember that songs and music are God's gift to us to help us express our adoration for his glory. Thinking about what songs to listen to and sing, is a little bit like choosing which part of the Bible to read for my devotionals. If I am always and only drawn to the great hymns of the faith, and frown every time a four-line chorus is put up on PowerPoint at church, I have to ask myself, 'Do I have nothing to learn about the glory of God from this chorus?'

Does God not delight in simple truths being repeated back to him with passion? Are the Psalms not full of just that kind of praise (Psalm 136 has the simple phrase 'his loves endures forever' repeated 26 times)? Does God not rejoice in the noise of electric guitar and drums and cymbals sounding out his glory, just as he rejoiced in the Old Testament?

> Praise him with the sounding of the trumpet, praise him with the harp and lyre, praise him with tambourine and dancing, praise him with the strings and flute, praise him with the clash of cymbals, praise him with resounding cymbals (Ps. 150:3-5).

Would we have told David to keep the volume down a bit, or sing something a bit more meaty? Am I not missing something of the glory of God if I frown every time a short chorus played with modern instruments is introduced in church?

Likewise if I frown every time a song written prior to 1990 is introduced in church, am I not guilty of the same editing of God? The wonderful thing about introducing a new generation to some of these older hymns is that they are so rich in teaching. *And Can It Be* is a hymn that contains such a rich variety of biblical truth with real emotional and musical power. The sheer wonder that God should save me through a cross, that the immortal God should chose to die, that he died for 'Adam's helpless race'. The glorious stirring of the music when we sing

> my chains fell off, my heart was free, I rose, went forth, and followed thee. Charles Wesley (1707–88) Trad.

The final heart-stopping vision of approaching God's throne, clothed with the righteousness of Christ, to receive the crown that Jesus will give his faithful ones – to live your life as a Christian and not sing that song many times, no matter what age you are, would be a tragedy.

Songs and hymns are a gift from God. When we combine the best of older hymns with meaningful newer songs that are more intimate and speak in today's language, we can grow in our daily appreciation of the full kaleidoscope of God's glory.

Let's be challenged both by the grandeur and depth of old hymns, and the intimacy and simplicity of newer songs, and not gravitate to one or the other because of personal taste. The Christian who is growing in their appreciation of God's glory, is the one who is constantly learning something new about him, and praising him for it.

4

Living for the Glory of God

Disciples with burning hearts know God for who he really is. Those who are most ready for a lifelong, passionate commitment to him, are those who have been awestruck by his majesty, terrified by his anger, captivated by his beauty, enchanted by his tenderness and left speechless by his mercy.

Our Bible reading, our prayer lives and exposure to the vast array of worship songs on offer, helps us to know God in all his splendour. But the Bible is clear, not just that we should appreciate his glory, but that we have a part to play in bringing glory to God.

The book of Ephesians shows this beautifully. Ephesians is divided into two parts. The first part (chapters 1 to 3) is the 'theology' of the book. It tells how God has called all kinds of people from eternity to be part of a single new community in Christ. Through the death of Jesus, God has reconciled us to himself (Eph. 2:1-10), and to each other (Eph. 2:11-22). People who have been reconciled to God and to each other, form this new community, the church that you and I are a part of – it's very exciting!

In fact Paul gets so excited about God's plans for you and me in the church that the first half of Ephesians ends with a doxology, a song of praise to God. Doxologies should really come at the end of books, but Paul jumps the gun. And Paul's doxology in Ephesians 3 finishes with these amazing words

> to him (God) be glory in the church and in Christ Jesus throughout all generations, for ever and ever! Amen. (Eph. 3:21)

This is a far-reaching verse that leaves you breathless when you understand its implications. The verse sums up God's plans for all creation, for the whole of eternity. It is a verse that sweeps across the whole of human time – 'throughout all generations' – and the whole of eternity 'for ever and ever'. In other words it sums up everything. The ultimate goal of God's plan, the reason why God does everything he ever does, is to be glorified for all time and for all eternity – 'to him be glory'.

Paul claims in this verse that God is glorified in two specific ways. First he is glorified 'in Christ'. That should not be a surprise to us. Hebrews tells us that Jesus is

> the radiance of God's glory and the exact representation of his being, sustaining all things by his powerful word (Heb. 1:3).

Jesus as the eternal Son of God, brought glory to God before he ever became a man. He is just like God in his nature, and in everything he does. He shares deity with God. He displays God's power and supremacy by keeping this whole universe running, simply under the authority of his Word.

When Jesus became a man, he brought glory to God in a whole new way. He obeyed God's will in everything he did. And his obedience finally led him to a cross. There are more ways than one to bring glory to God. The Bible seems to suggest that Jesus brought even more glory to God through his humble, ignominious death as a man, than he did as the Son who upholds the universe. The Bible makes much more of the blood that Jesus shed as a man on the cross, than it does of Jesus' power to uphold the heavens.

The book of Revelation is full of songs of praise to Jesus for the very human way that he achieved our salvation. Jesus is worthy to receive the praise of the angels, because he obeyed God to the point of death

> You are worthy to take the scroll
> and to open its seals,
> because you were slain,
> and with your blood you
> purchased men for God
> from every tribe and language
> and people and nation (Rev. 5:9).

God was truly honoured by Jesus' sacrifice. God's plan of salvation came to fulfilment when Jesus offered his body to die in shame. And that is a very important point for us to realize as we think about the second way God is glorified in this verse.

God is glorified in you

The fact that Jesus could bring so much glory to God is hardly surprising. Of course God will take pleasure in his perfect Son. But the *way* in which Jesus brought God glory *as a man on earth* is a powerful challenge and encouragement for us. His life on earth brought glory to God, not because he flung stars into space, or presided over an army of angels. He brought glory to God in very human ways that you and I can share in.

He offered his body to God, and that is exactly what Paul invites us ordinary men and women to do as an expression of our worship to him.

> I urge you, my brothers, in view of God's mercies, to offer your bodies as living sacrifices, holy and pleasing to God – this is your spiritual act of worship (Rom. 12:1).

I don't need special divine powers to glorify God. I can simply offer my body to him. I can give him my time, my talents, my energy, my thought life and even my money. God is glorified not just 'in Christ Jesus', but in the very human 'church'. I can bring God glory by loving my wife in the same way Jesus loves the church – he gave himself for her. If I give myself up for my wife, in a multitude of different ways every day, from being available when the chores are being done, to really listening and facilitating her hopes and ambitions, then I am glorifying God.

If I have the self-discipline to be 'holy', then I am bringing God glory. 'Holy' simply means set apart for God's purposes. Jesus showed his holiness by setting aside the personal fame, and pleasure he could have received from the people who were pining to make him king, so that he could drive himself towards the cross on which God was asking him to die.

In just the same way, I can glorify God by setting aside personal pleasure and the wish to be popular, recognized or successful, so that I can obey God's call on my life. That may be a call to ease off on my career aspirations to give more time to serving in church. It may be a call to two weeks' summer beach *mission* rather than two weeks' summer beach *holiday*; to reading challenging Christian books rather than watching *EastEnders*; to sending emails of encouragement to Christian friends rather than surfing the net for entertainment; spending less time in shopping malls, and more time in the Scriptures.

Jesus' life on earth proves to us that we can bring glory to God in a multitude of practical ways, every day. God wants to be glorified 'in the church' as well as 'in Christ Jesus'. Are we robbing him of the glory he deserves, or are we prepared to give ourselves up for his glory? Our problem is less finding a way to glorify God, and more having a will to glorify God. Bringing glory to him is costly – the image of Jesus' cross magnifies the cost in bold letters. But cross carrying Christians, like Colosseum Christians, bring glory to God in very human, practical ways.

The doorway to satisfaction

But there is a strange joy that comes from laying your body on God's altar. Paul says we can feel God's power surging through us, as we fulfil the reason we were created (Col. 1:29). We were created to bring God glory through these bodies he has given us. We become partners with God in fulfilling his chief desire – to be glorified. God responds to the worship that our sacrifice creates, and we feel his pleasure as we lay down our lives. This is *'the secret of the burning heart'* – to feel the pleasure of God burning within us, as we lay down our lives for his eternal glory.

The American pastor John Piper has become quite controversial in Christian circles by referring to what he calls 'Christian hedonism'. Hedonism is not a word we would normally associate with burning-heart Christians. Hedonism is the pursuit of pleasure. Usually when we think about hedonism we imagine a group of eighteen to thirties getting drunk and partying the night away on some beach in Ibiza. Hedonism seems to stand in sharp contrast to the holy, self-sacrificial life we normally associate with being a disciple. But Dr Piper provides a compelling case that Christians should be 'spiritual pleasure seekers'(*Desiring God*, Oregon: Multnomah, 1996). Piper's motto is clear

> God is most glorified in us, when we are most satisfied in him.

If bringing glory to God is the reason we were created in the first place, then it stands to reason that we are at our best as human beings when we are fulfilling our calling. Have you ever felt God's pleasure burn within you as you have served him in some way and brought him glory? Have you ever felt that strange delight the first disciples felt when they were being called upon even to suffer for him in the early days of the church when persecution was the norm?

> The apostles left . . . rejoicing because they had been counted worthy of suffering disgrace for the Name (Acts 5:41).

There was something about glorifying God that made even suffering seem joyful to these ordinary men whose lives had been captured by the cause of the Kingdom.

Rejoicing in suffering seems the ultimate contradiction of our sensitive, frail humanity. And yet when the glory of God is our goal, we can feel God's pleasure even when we're facing opposition for our Christian commitment.

God's glory v. my glory

Here then is the first delight of the Christian whose heart will burn forever. He thinks about, dreams about, feels for, and places his body on the line, for the glory of God. There is a sense in which this book could finish right here. If our hearts (our entire beings) are caught up with the glory of God, then there is enough spiritual fuel in that passion to light up our whole lives now and forever.

The rest of this book will unpack the three other 'chambers' of the burning heart – 'God's people', 'God's world', and 'God's return'. But these three passions are a reflection of God's glory. God is glorified in us when we love his people, when we have a desire to reach his world, and when we live urgent lives longing for his return. The glory of God is an umbrella that covers all areas of authentic Christian living.

What we need to do right now is make a list of all the things that our hearts are longing for, that clash with a desire for God's glory. Can we be honest about this? I know deep down that my desire to be recognized and appreciated by all as a dynamic Christian leader, leads in some way every day to a headlong collision with my desire to glorify God.

The two desires are incompatible. And I sometimes fool myself into believing that I will be more thrilled if I am awarded the prize of 'Most valuable Christian leader of the twenty-first century' before an adoring church holding up palm branches and blowing kisses, than I would be if I hear 'Well done!' one day in paradise from the glorious lips of the Creator and Saviour of the universe. What a fool I am!

But just occasionally I catch a glimpse in my life of what bringing glory to God means to the Lord of Glory himself. Just occasionally, when I'm holding the hand of an eighty-year-old cancer patient who can't remember my name, and I'm praying with sincerity that God will give this man the grace to endure these last few hours before the Gates of Splendour open to him.

Just then, I can almost see the smile of God. And I know at that moment, this is why I was made. And nothing in all the heavens can possibly compare to the inescapable delight of pleasing the King of Angels.

But I have to take time deliberately and constantly every day to confess the desires in my heart that run contrary to his glory, and then with real seriousness set my mind 'on things above, where Christ is seated at the right hand of God' (Col. 3:1). What are the desires in your heart that are stealing away a heart that burns for God's glory? Is it the desire to be recognized? Is it career ambitions? Is it 'Being the best parent the world has ever known'? Is it the desire for deep intimacy and friendship with another human being? Is it money? Is it alcohol? Is it Sky TV? Is it . . .?

Whatever they are confess them openly and seriously to God today. Tell him that you want your heart to burn for his glory alone. Tell him you're discovering that is why he made you in the first place. Ask his forgiveness for the wasted ambitions that have turned you into a 'disappointed disciple'. Get on your knees right now and ask him to fill you with a longing to bring him glory in your thoughts, your dreams, your emotions, your body.

Living for the Glory of God

Ask him to encourage you in lots of little ways every day that he is answering your prayer, and keep praying that prayer as you start each day for the rest of your life.

Review

- God's primary passion, from which all other passions derive, is a passion for his own glory. We need to rediscover the full kaleidoscope of God's glory, and not edit him, or make him into a lesser god than he really is to suit our tastes.
- That means adoring God for his dangerous qualities of burning holiness and absolute justice, as well as his more endearing qualities of compassion and grace.
- When we worship God for who he truly is, by an appreciation of the full wonder of his character as revealed in his Word, and cultivated through prayer and Christian songs, our hearts start to burn.
- Just as Jesus brought glory to God in very human ways, we too can glorify him by laying our lives down as living sacrifices to him.

For personal study

- Why is a proper understanding of God's glory so important for our spiritual growth?
- Chapter 2 mentions several ways we can 'edit' God (the austere god, the inoffensive god, the packaged god). What do you feel most threatens your understanding of God's glory? What can you do to guard against editing God in this way?
- Note down specific ways you can develop your understanding of the full 'kaleidoscope' of God's glory, in the following areas:

- Your reading of Scripture
- Your prayer life
- Your exposure to Christian music
• What are the ambitions in your heart which clash with the desire to bring God glory? What specific action do you need to take to put God first?
• Chapter 3 describes how Jesus was able to glorify God in very human ways. In what specific ways do you feel you can glorify God in your life at the moment?

Part Three:
Second Chamber: A Heart that Burns for God's People

5

The Whole New Meaning of 'Love'

Love one another as I have loved you (Jn. 15:12).

'The church would be great if it wasn't for people!' You have probably heard that quip before. Most of us have a lot less trouble with the idea of loving God than we do loving other Christians. God is committed to me, Christians are self-centred. God is consistent, Christians wear masks of sickly sweetness on a Sunday morning, then tear my character apart over coffee on a Monday. God is worth the greatest effort of my soul – Christians aren't worth the buttons on my shirt. 'The church would be great if it wasn't for people!'

There is nothing more deflating than to sit with a mature Christian couple who are pouring out their broken hearts to you because of how they have been treated by other believers. Some of the breaches of trust, the pettiness, the name calling that goes on between mature Christians, often in the name of defending truth, are a damning indictment of the Christ we confess.

If we are to have burning hearts, we need to be caught up with the passions of God. And God's primary passion, which stems from a passion for his own glory, is his passion for 'the church'. God describes his love affair with his chosen people in the most lofty language. We are the apple of his eye, his sons and daughters, heirs of his inheritance, his personal possession, even his bride.

For some fathomless reason that exists only in the secret counsels of the Trinity, the Father forced himself to cut off all links with his beautiful Son during three hours of Calvary darkness, because he loves, he absolutely adores, he swoons over a group of erratic, fragile people called 'the church'.

A new commandment

On his way to the darkness of Calvary, the beautiful Son had only a few hours of teaching left to give to his motley crew of well-meaning but often pig-headed disciples. How would the King of Glory use those last precious words? What great element of God's passions and plans would Jesus leave behind as a lasting treasure to be remembered and preached and meditated on above any other of his golden words?

The dramatic centrepiece of that last teaching session with his disciples is an unrestricted command aimed at all generations of his followers.

> My command is this: Love each other as I have loved you (Jn. 15:12).

Mark Twain once said, 'It is not the things I don't understand in the Bible than trouble me, it's the things I do!' Here is the simplest, clearest command in all of the Bible, that even a child could understand. These are words I have known all my life, but watching Mel Gibson's movie *The Passion of the Christ* brought them home to me more powerfully than ever before. In the movie, as the soldiers are graphically hammering the nails into his hands and feet (there are 'no holds barred' in the special effects), the scene suddenly shifts back to the upper room, and these lovely words of the Master. How are we to love one another? We are to love in the manner in which Jesus has loved us – the rugged picture of nails in his hands and feet is a poignant symbol of the lengths we ought to go in our love.

I'm sure as John the disciple watched that horrific event unfold before his eyes, the haunting words of Jesus on the previous evening must have come flooding back with new power. As he stared with tear-stained eyes at Jesus' broken body, he must have thought, 'so this is how I am to love God's people'. Tradition goes that, many years later John, now an old man, would mumble those words repeatedly every time he met with God's people – 'love one another!' much to the annoyance of other Christians he met with.

But what appeared to be the tired mumblings of a man past his prime, are actually the heartbeat of the gospel. The cross cemented Jesus' teaching the previous night in a way that John would never forget. The centre-piece of the First Letter of John has this exact same command, as though the cross was just as fresh and penetrating in John's imagination

> This is the message you heard from the beginning:
> We should love one another (1 Jn. 3:11).

If we are to be captivated by the passions of God, to feel what he feels, think how he thinks, and act how he acts, then we cannot divorce ourselves from this pivotal command. The road to a burning heart is not just a heart that burns for God's glory, but a heart that burns for God's people who matter to him so very much.

The figures I read recently from George Barna, the Christian statistician, only confirmed what we already know instinctively. More people leave the church for lack of love than for any other reason. I am a pastor who spends a great deal of time trying to shape and improve his sermons. Enormous efforts are often put into compiling a Sunday worship service that is clear and compelling – songs, interviews, dramas, the message all blending together into a seamless masterpiece. But how much time and effort do we put into the very reason why most people won't be there on a Sunday to see it all?

Detached lives

Perhaps the biggest obstacle that Christians face to obeying this command, is the detached lives we have chosen to live. This truth came home to me most forcibly as my wife and I were looking for a new house recently. The most desirable houses are those which are farthest away from others. A detached house adds greatly to its value because that is the kind of life we crave.

If our hedges and walls are high, if we can look out at nothing but grass and fields, if we can ensure that no surrounding neighbour gets a 'look in', then we have found paradise. Detachment is not just clear in the homes we chose to live in – the huge advancements in the world of personal electronics and gadgetry, have simply emphasized our alienation from each other. We can live most of our lives without a reference to anyone else.

Bedrooms of teenagers equipped with the latest in video games, satellite TV systems, and a virtual music studio mean that they can disappear into their own world. The bedroom door becomes a fence to the rest of the family, and the room itself a cocoon from the outside world. The microwave generation has destroyed family meal times – TV dinners are best-sellers in supermarkets. The thought of a family eating together at the table while parents and children talk, laugh and even pray together about their day, now seems a quaint walk down memory lane to a 'prehistoric' 1950s world that is now as lost as the dinosaurs.

If we are detached from family, we are positively alienated from the outside world. What used to be a visit to the local butcher or grocer, that would inevitably have involved a chat with him, has now been swallowed up by giant supermarkets. One of the biggest supermarkets in the country has recently opened near my home. It is incredible that you can walk around an entire building containing over one thousand people, without hearing a single conversation. Today's massive supermarkets are built around speed and customer satisfaction, not around relationships. If you breathe a 'good morning' to the lady at the till, as she 'beeps' an endless array of items, you feel that you've 'gone deep'!

Offices have been taken over by 'machine speak'. We may feel like we are communicating to each other via email, but it's an illusion. We descend into email speak. I have stopped writing 'Dear' at the beginning of emails because it wastes too much time. How many emails zoom around the globe with all the personal warmth of 'Roger, Report attached, Dave'? There is a vast amount of information being shared, but you can't look into someone's eyes on an email. You can't touch their shoulder, or hear their voice, sense their vulnerability, or warm their heart. Electronic relationships are a poor substitute for the real thing.

The gospel is relational

What a contrast our detached lives are to God's plans for his creation. Christians have lulled themselves into thinking that individual faith is all that matters. We talk with joy about 'my own personal Saviour'. Implicit in this statement is privatized religion. I can live out my faith in Jesus without anyone else's help. It's safer that way anyway. If I try to get close to too many people, they may compromise my faith.

Because of our individualistic religion, we totally misunderstand the Bible's teaching on holiness. We have made holiness simply about my behaviour with my God – no one else has to be involved. I can rigorously pursue my Christian disciplines of private prayer and private devotion in 'hermitville', and be holy. After all, the word holy means 'set apart'. That suits my lifestyle down to the ground. But biblical holiness is built around relationships.

We get so upset with the Bible when it talks about a father's sins being passed down to his children, or the whole community of Israel being judged because of Achan's sin (Josh. 7) – why on earth did God tell the nation to stone Achan's whole family for the sin of one man? Relationships with each other are an integral part of our relationship with God. We struggle with the doctrine of 'original sin' where I am counted guilty because of Adam's sin – my relationship to Adam seems unusually important to God.

Relationships and the gospel

Our problem stems from a limited understanding of the cross. Ephesians 2 is a chapter that contains both the gospel we believe and the gospel we don't want to believe. We love Ephesians 2:1-10 – it seems the ultimate in privatized religion. God has rescued me from the snare of the world, flesh and devil (vv.1-3). He has lifted me up and seated me in heavenly realms (vv. 4-7). I am saved by grace, not works (vv. 8-9), and I am now becoming God's work of art (v.10). This is the gospel we believe – I have been reconciled to God.

What we fail to realize is that the 'you' of Ephesians 2:1 is in the plural. It is *we* who lived in the world, *we* who are seated with Christ, *we* who have been saved by grace, and *we* who are becoming works of art. If you remove relationships from the gospel, there is precious little left. The second part of Ephesians 2 is the gospel we fail to adequately grasp. God's whole plan in sending Christ was not only to reconcile us as individuals to himself, but also to reconcile us to each other. Relationships are at the heart of the gospel message.

Christ's death has 'destroyed the barrier, the dividing wall of hostility' that used to separate Jews from Gentiles. And the reuniting of Jew and Gentile is a picture of the re-uniting of all humanity. Paul states this truth in a beautiful, liberating way in Galatians 3

> There is neither Jew nor Greek, slave nor free, male nor female, for you are all one in Christ Jesus (Gal. 3:28).

This is the gospel. I vividly remember sitting in a huge tent in the Keswick Convention when I was a teenager. I had come from a very small Brethren church in Northern Ireland, and this was my first time at a big church event. Behind the speaker on the platform was this wonderful text in bold letters, 'All one in Christ Jesus'.

I looked around me to see people of all ages, both sexes, several different nationalities standing together as a symphony of praise to God. A sense of elation ran through my whole body. So this was God's plan for the church. A new humanity in Christ coming together to encourage and spur each other on to live for the world to come. What a vision.

The New Testament and relationships

It amazes me the amount of space in the New Testament that is devoted to issues of relationship. To live as though we do not need each other is to take Tipp-Ex to half of the Epistles. Quite apart from Jesus' profound love ethic in the Gospels, and the ultimate expression of love on the cross – the pinnacle moment in the history of the universe – the rest of the New Testament positively pulsates with issues of relationships.

In Acts, Luke seems to be saying that the church was at its best when 'they broke bread together', when they 'shared everything in common', when 'they enjoyed the favour of all the people'. Deacons enter the church because of a relationship problem – the Greek widows were being left out of the distribution of food in favour of Hebraic widows. We wonder why the author is at pains to point out this issue when we want to continue the passionate stories of the church's preaching in its early years – it seems relationships were important.

The Whole New Meaning of 'Love'

The biggest threat and most profound blessing for the church was Paul's relationship with the church. The story of 'Saul the slayer' becoming 'Paul the preacher' was hard for the first Christians to swallow. His conversion was greeted by the church with understandable suspicion, but it is wise Barnabas who takes the fledgling apostle under his wing, and vouches for him to the Jerusalem apostles. What a decisive step forward that was for the history of the church.

The crisis meeting of the Jerusalem council (Acts 15) was essentially a matter of relationships between Jews and Gentiles – how could Gentiles be integrated into the church without upsetting Jews? Relationships are at the heart of the church's evangelism strategy. Paul talks to Lydia on a river bank, develops meaningful friendships with Priscilla and Aquila, with Tyrannus who loans him a lecture hall, with Erastus in Corinth who had an important role in the local council.

The biggest stumbling blocks to the gospel again revolve around relationships. Paul and Barnabas have an acrimonious split over the desertion of Mark (whose company Paul later longs for in prison in Ephesus, see 2 Timothy 4).

But it is in Paul's letters, which we hold to be the quintessential in 'sound doctrine', where relationships seem most crucial. Romans, a book best known for its sound doctrine, finishes with a whole chapter of names – the preacher's nightmare. Paul seems familiar with an extraordinary number of people in a church he has never visited.

He knows Phoebe as a 'great help to many people'; Priscilla and Aquila as 'fellow-workers', who risked their lives for him; Epenetus as 'my dear friend' and his 'first convert'; Andronicus and Junias as fellow prisoners;

others in the chapter as dear friends; Apelles as 'approved in Christ'; Herodion as 'my relative'; Tryphena and Tryphosa as those who 'work hard in the Lord'; Rufus as a 'chosen in the Lord', and that is only a summary.

Paul knows more people in a church he has never been to, than I know people in the church I have spent most of my life in. Surely that says something profound to our detached generation about the priority the apostle placed on spiritual relationships.

Paul's long-distance relationships

Corinthians contains battles between leaders, false apostles creating personal trouble for Paul, the public discipline of a man whose immorality was affecting the whole church, a warning to mature Christians not to damage a 'weaker brother', and of course, the supreme exposition of love (1 Cor. 13). Galatians is a response to the internal strife caused by Judaizers, who were spreading confusion among the believers. It calls us to demonstrate the highly relational fruit of the Spirit ('love, joy, peace, patience, kindness, goodness, faithfulness, gentleness and self-control', Gal. 5:22,23) and to 'Carry each other's burdens' (Gal. 6:2).

Ephesians presents us with the most profound theology of Jew and Gentile being united in Christ within a new humanity reconciled to God and each other. Philippians is all about the need for humility in church relationships (the beautiful 'Christ hymn' of Phil. 2:5-11 is really a call for Christians to show humility to each other), and it calls for Euodia and Syntyche, obviously two outstanding women of the faith, to agree with each other.

The Whole New Meaning of 'Love'

Colossians, like Ephesians, has a powerful 'one body' theology, profound teaching for husbands and wives and lengthy greetings from Paul's fellow workers. Thessalonians reveals Paul sharing his life as a pastor in front of the church, as a mother caring for her children and as a father urging them on to holy living. And we haven't even arrived at the most personal, relationship driven books of the whole New Testament.

Paul's letters to Timothy, Titus and Philemon are built on his profound relationship with fellow ministers and church leaders. The whole letter of Philemon is about a relationship rupture between a master and his slave. Paul uses his relationship with Philemon to provoke reconciliation, while Onesimus' life is saved through Paul's loving concern for the kind of runaway who would be left adrift by many of our churches.

Paul's tears for Timothy, the way he shaped Timothy as a fellow missionary, the time he devoted to him in the midst of a hectic ministry life, are powerful expressions of what we should mean to each other as Christians. It is an intense, discipleship-based, counter-cultural, inter-generational relationship that provokes some of the most moving language in Scripture – 'I have no-one else like him' (Phil. 2:20).

There is no fuller expression in the Bible of what one Christian can do for another as they love each other, share each other's burdens, pray for each other, and live as co-workers for the gospel. This is the kind of relationship that God intends for us, to spur us on in our Christian lives.

6

The Issues We Can't Avoid

How we relate to each other is the heartbeat of loving God and living for his glory. The whole message of Scripture, from the Garden of Eden to the heavenly city, is a story of God reconciling people to himself, and reconciling people to each other so that we might love each other with the same unqualified commitment that God shows to us. 'God is love', and if we are to become anything like the God we confess, love ought to be our highest priority and deepest desire.

As with most good theology, the problem is less with accepting it and more with how we put it into practice. It is one thing to be convinced that 'love one another' is one of God's central passions. It is one thing to recognize that if I am ever to have a burning heart, my heart needs to burn for God's people as much as it burns for him. Or to put it a better way, loving other people is one of the clearest ways we show God we love him. But I can hear you ask 'have you really seen some of the "one anothers" in my church?

'Do you know my past history of hurt and suspicion and family feuds – the back-stabbing, the snide looks, the lies and "not-speaking-to-each-other" rows we have had over the years, all sugar-coated behind our Sunday worship decorum? Can you not "beam me up" out of this current group of "one anothers" where there is no hope, and place me in another group where I can start from scratch?'

Sadly, our Lord rarely offers us that utopia. 'Love' in the Bible has always been a messy word. Real love is hammered out on the anvil of human sinfulness. If we are truly honest with ourselves, one of the greatest barriers to experiencing true, apostolic community is us. Even Paul and Barnabas, two of the most passionate, God-fearing, heart-burning disciples who ever lived, had such heated words with each other, despite their long history of friendship, that they parted company. The same man who desired to love more than he desired to 'speak in the tongues of men and of angels' (1 Cor. 13:1), knew that he had to learn to love in an imperfect world, where he was part of the problem.

No, God will not lift you out of your current church relationships to allow you to practise burning heart love. It has to start right where you are with Sally who called you 'two-faced', Jim who appears to be as cold as a fish, Dave whose social skills rival Mr Bean's and you, who still harbour grudges against them all. If Jesus' love was tested by Thomas' doubting, Peter's denial, and Judas' kiss, then should I expect an easier ride from fellow believers?

Love is more an act of will

The Bible's perspective on authentic Christian love becomes very helpful when we're faced with the Sallys,

Jims and Daves of this world. When we talk about having a heart that burns for other Christians, we are not calling for a frothy, huggy kind of response to each other during a church service. Nor are we suggesting that we simply overlook the unfortunate side of each other's personality. As Christians we are called to deal with reality as it is, not to live in some kind of 'super spiritual' dream world.

What we are suggesting is much more meaningful, and costly. It begins not with asking the question 'Is there anything I find appealing about this person?' There may well not be. Love in the Bible seems less to do with my instinctive feelings towards a person, and more to do with my longing for that person's well-being in Christ.

The list of people we mentioned from Romans 16 is a case in point. This whole list of names that Paul trots out, are people he is deeply concerned for almost as a father is concerned for a child. I doubt whether Paul would have felt equally at home in the presence of all these people. Would he have felt all warm and fuzzy about taking Apollos out for a social drink on a Friday night? Somehow I doubt that.

Paul's love is expressed by a longing for the spiritual development of these believers. Paul's burning heart for other Christians is a very natural extension of his love for Christ. He wants to see these men and women become fully mature for Christ, and he prays, he yearns for their spiritual development. He rejoices in their spiritual progress, and weeps over their backsliding. Love between Christians is not a superficial hug but a profound longing that each person in my sphere of influence might experience the fullness of Christ in their lives, as they strive for his Kingdom.

That vision is the overwhelming passion that drives Paul to visit with people until late into the night. He carries their burdens and teaches them with tears. He prays for them with longing, and openly shares his life with them. He even rebukes them when that is necessary, because his heart burns for them. He is like a mother in the pains of childbirth until Christ is formed in them. What a heart grabbing image that is for us to pursue in our lives.

As an expectant mother willingly endures the most personal pain in order to see her vulnerable child grow, so God calls us to long for each other's spiritual growth.

Is that not a compelling reflection of the love God has for us? He loved us while we were still sinners, not because our sin was attractive to him – perish the thought. He loved us because his heart longed for us to be like the Son of his delight. He made us in his image. His first creation was 'very good'. Reflecting the beauty of Christ was what God desired for us deep in his being since before the world began. He grieves that his image within us has been tarnished by the Fall.

God longs with a limitless love, that Christ would be formed in us. What a glorious thought. The culmination of God's longing for us will be revealed at the very moment we see the Lord face to face for the first time

> we know that when he appears, we shall be like him, for we shall see him as he is (1 Jn. 3:2).

Catching God's vision

What might happen in our often wounded, grieving churches, if we repented before God for our detached lives? What transformation might occur if we became convicted about God's vision for his church to reflect this counter-cultural love in front of a watching world? What revival might break out if we earnestly prayed for the kind of Spirit-filled longing for each other that would bring a taste of heaven to earth? Nothing that we pursue in our Christian lives matters as much as this, because nothing more closely reflects the character of God and his plan of redemption from eternity to eternity – that we might love as we have been loved.

Let's not dare beat our drums about Calvinism and Arminianism, our position on baptism or the second coming, our disputes over spiritual gifts and the role of women, before we plead with our burning heart for God to teach us how to love each other in Christ's name. If the stable of Bethlehem, the basin and the towel of the upper room, the sweat of Gethsemane, the nails and spear of Calvary, and the folded sheets of the empty tomb mean anything to us, they should move our hearts to long for each other as Christ has longed and sweated and cried, and prayed and bled and conquered for us.

> A new command I give you . . . As I have loved you, so you must love one another (Jn. 13:34).

It's a clear sign of my corruption that I am often more determined to win a theological argument (or any kind of argument) than I am to burn with longing for a brother or sister in Christ. I am more determined to be seen as 'right' in everyone's eyes, than I am to back down in an argument for the sake of love, which is a much higher calling than any other argument I could possibly win.

The fact that churches have split over issues ranging from 'which leader do we approve of' to 'what kind of carpet do we put down in the sanctuary' shows that we have taken God's most beautiful flower, and trampled its petals into the ground. This love that longs for Christ likeness in other believers matters infinitely more than whatever colour of carpet I walk on into church.

It matters more than which hymn book we sing from or whether we raise our hands during the service. It is supremely more important than the form of baptism we espouse, or the version of the Bible we read from. It is more important than the practice or otherwise of charismatic gifts in the church. It matters more than amillenialism, premillenialism, postmillenialism or all the 'isms' put together.

This love matters as much as the blood of the cross itself, because it is the blood and the cost of Calvary that provokes our hearts to burn with longing for each other, and prove in our congregations that his blood was worth it. That he did not die for wretches who would remain wretches forever. He died so that his supreme, fathomless, longing love might bloom in our hearts.

I am not saying that all these doctrinal matters are not important. They are of central importance in a day when doctrine is being frowned upon as irrelevant and dull. I am simply saying that we would deal with doctrine in a much more God pleasing way in our churches, if all our discussions were bathed in this kind of longing love for each other. To quote a popular song, 'Love changes everything!'

Love begins at home

If we are convinced that one of the passions that lights up God's heart is a loving longing for Christ to be formed in us, then our hearts will only burn if we embrace that passion for ourselves. The burning heart is a heart that longs to see Christ formed in others. But this is not some vague theological principle for us to tick off in our list of beliefs. Longing love is very practical. Before we try and practise this love at church, we need to practise it at home.

Home life is often the hardest place for our hearts to burn for each other. As husbands and wives, parents and children we are so used to seeing each other's 'rougher edges'. We are so used to living with each other, speaking to each other in our most familiar, earthy language, we become so accustomed to fits of rage and moodiness with each other, that home can seem the last place to practise burning heart love.

But if we take the New Testament's teaching on marriage and the home seriously, we have to burn among our 'nearest and dearest' before we ever burn in our church. If we are longing for Christ to shine in the hearts of our brothers and sisters at church, but are careless at home, we have our priorities wrong.

As a husband myself, perhaps it is best to talk to husbands here especially. If you are like me, often you give yourself so much to Christians outside the home, that your wife gets the dregs of your burning heart. Somehow we feel our job is to love everyone apart from the partner God has given us to love and shape and influence uniquely – our wife. We often see home as a place to 'chill out', to let your hair down, the only real place I can 'be myself'. But what we really mean by that is that home is the place for me to be lazy and lacklustre, sinking into my couch with the remote control in my hand. Burning-heart love is rarely to be found at home, where it ought to count the most.

We find it easier to pray with other Christians in our church building or home group because that is the place we are expected to pray. But do we pray with and for our wives? Is this special individual that God has placed in my life for me to bless and inspire and encourage, is she the first focus of my burning heart? I'm not talking about romance here. I'm saying, does discipleship come into your marriage? Do you long for Christ to be formed in your wife? If you don't, then here is an excellent place to be a real man and start practising real love.

A husband is to love his wife 'as Christ loved the church'. As a husband I am to 'sanctify' my wife, just as Christ sanctifies the church. Her holiness ought to be my deepest concern. As husbands we have more of an opportunity to promote Christ-likeness in our wives than in any other person, because we spend so much time together, and can talk on a deeper level than in other relationships that are marked by more formality.

Husbands, let me ask you, when was the last time you asked your wife how she was feeling? When was the last time you sat down with her and gave her your full attention, allowing her to unpack her heart, and share her dreams with you? When was the last time you asked her to pray with you, or read the Bible with you? When was the last time you put down the remote control to serve her – to change a light bulb, or empty the rubbish, or hoover the floor, or scrub the toilets (without being asked)? There are a myriad of ways to say to your wife 'I love you', but as men we so often live our lives blind to our wives, until bedtime when we want them to suddenly 'switch on' and meet our needs.

At the end of your life, will your wife be more godly because she's spent her life with you? Will you be able to present her to her heavenly husband, Christ, as a beautiful bride, adorned by her good works, her fervent prayers, her meaningful ministry in church? Will she remember you as an enabler, an inspirer, as well as a lover? Are you just as interested in her inner beauty, as you are in her outer beauty? Which do you talk about more? Your wife has been entrusted to you, so that you can enable her to flourish as a woman of God. Don't think about saving other peoples' souls, before you save your wife!

And wives, how will you inspire Christ-likeness in your husband? In the husbands and wives passage in Ephesians 5:22-33, while the emphasis is on husbands 'loving' their wives sacrificially, it's interesting that wives are called to 'respect' their husbands. It is very tempting for a wife to try and mould her husband into who she wants him to be, rather than what God wants him to be.

But wives can be real discipleship partners with their husbands if they take every opportunity they can to encourage their husbands in their God-given role. Show your respect for your husband by looking to him in his role as head of the home (Eph. 5:33; 1 Cor. 11:3). Your husband is much more likely to rise to his calling as a Christ-like spouse in your marriage, if you praise him for his good qualities, rather than highlighting his faults. What a delightful thing it is for a wife to 'build up' her husband towards godliness.

What about the children?

And do we have this loving longing for our children? It is probably true that every Christian parent has instinctive longings for their children, but are our longings misplaced? Do we long for them to be godly, more than we long for them to be safe? Do we long for them to be righteous more than we long for them to get married or have a good career?

I remember hearing Dr Tony Campolo preaching at a Christian Union meeting a few years ago. He spoke about the longings of American and Japanese parents for their children. Statistics showed that American parents wanted their children above all to be 'happy', while the Japanese wanted their offspring to be 'successful'.

Campolo challenged us in his uniquely passionate style, that neither 'happy' nor 'successful' was a high enough longing for our children. We should long for them to be 'holy'. We should long for them to be like Jesus, and we should be dissatisfied, frustrated, urgent in prayer for them, even if they achieve all the happiness of the world, without passionately pursuing the Lord.

I have seen many Christian parents just beaming about their Jonny who has just become a doctor, or their Amy who has passed the bar exam. And then you ask the awkward question, 'And how are they doing with the Lord?' and there is almost an embarrassed hush. 'Well, Jonny just moved in with a non-Christian girl, but she's a lovely girl, she really is. She'll be good for him!'

'Amy hasn't been to church for a few weeks, but you know her law firm is very demanding and it's important she gets a good start.' I would love to sit and pray with those parents with longing for their children to pursue Christ with the same passion they are pursuing other things. But often the Christian parents have been more excited by the worldly success and shallow 'happiness' of their children, and may feel less comfortable if their children had burning hearts, but were struggling socially and career wise.

May God help me to have godly longings for my children as they grow up. I won't be able to control how they respond to Jesus and the gospel, but I pray that they at least will be able to gauge my profound longings for them to walk with Jesus.

Deuteronomy challenges us to bring God's commands into our homes, to talk about them with our children, to make Christ-centred conversation as common in our homes as meal times and homework. It is a great practice to set aside time, perhaps after the evening meal, for the whole family to gather together, just for ten minutes or so, to read a passage from the Bible, discuss it for a moment and then pray. That 'ten-minutes-a-day' commitment teaches our children that Christ is the centre of our homes, and whatever other longings we have for their lives, we most long for them to pursue Christ with all their hearts. It does not take much imagination or creativity to have a family reading, just a longing for our children to have burning hearts.

Christian friendship v. discipleship relationships

One of the most profound ways we can start to long for each other 'in Christ', is by having a new vision for the natural friendships we develop in the church family. What I said previously about getting on with the Sallys, Daves and Jims of this world is, of course, not true of every Christian relationship. I'm sure we all have 'natural' friends in church – people we instinctively like. People who share our passions, even our hobbies. The kind of people we would chose to invite to a birthday celebration or a special meal for select friends. What do we long for in their lives?

Often we are so happy to find such a natural friend among other Christians that we don't want to spoil that friendship by getting all 'religious' with them. There is someone I like to talk 'football' with. I'll even go round to his house to watch a Champion's League match on Sky.

The Issues We Can't Avoid 71

But somehow the thought of talking to him about Christ seems alien, almost embarrassing, even though he is a believer.

Perhaps there is a woman in church whom you really 'click' with. You'll go on shopping trips with her, you'll chat to her about your favourite movies at the cinema, and even buy her kids birthday presents because you are used to being in her home. But the thought of intentionally praying with her is far from your mind. If you get all 'spiritual' with her it may destroy that friendship that has come to mean a lot to you.

There is a world of difference between having a Christian friend, and entering a discipleship relationship with that person. And yet natural friendship is such a powerful building block to 'spur each other on towards love and good deeds' (Heb. 10:25). What is your friendship based on if it isn't based on Christ? Is there not something missing in your Christian friendship if that relationship does not lead you to long for that person in Christ?

Some of the most inspiring moments of church I have experienced are when a group of young men get together quite naturally to talk about the Bible. It's nothing that the church has organized. The Pastor has not mentioned it. It's simply a group of young men who happen to get on really well with each other, and use that natural friendship to inspire each other on in Christ. That really is spontaneous Christian love at work.

I have seen groups of six to eight men who talk together honestly about their work struggles, not to have a moaning session, but to pray for each other. Because they are close friends, they share issues in their lives they would not feel comfortable sharing with anyone else, with the aim of growing in Christ. They become accountable to each other. They are a tight-knit group, who keep confidentiality a high priority, and who open up to each other about their struggles with the Christian life. Have I become lazy with my devotional life? How am I handling my money? How am I dealing with sexual temptation? What am I doing on business trips away from home, or with my TV watching habits?

They meet together once a month on a Saturday. They study theology together in a relaxed environment, they read one chapter per month of a discipleship book together and pray. It's not rocket science. It's Christian love in action. It's realizing that God gave us to each other not just for friendship but to drive each other on in Christ. What are our friendships based on if they don't inspire us to be more for Christ than we could ever be on our own? I think those groups excite God. I think he's glad he founded something called 'church' when he sees a group of young men whose friendship in Christ means enough to them that they long for each other to be more like Jesus. What a vision for the church.

The power of home groups

Probably the most fruitful forum for developing discipleship relationships is through 'home group's. Home groups are the perfect soil for genuine Christian love to sprout.

While the early church in Acts 2 used to have large congregational gatherings in the temple courts for their public witness, they would combine that with meeting much more informally 'in their homes' (Acts 2:46) where they shared each others' lives on a daily basis. The book of Philemon begins by Paul greeting Philemon and 'the church that meets in your home' (Phlm. 2). Some of the most powerful days of the church occurred long before the formality of steeples and chapel bells.

The 'ordinariness' of inter-generational home groups forces people to pull down social barriers and be real with one another. It somehow feels more appropriate to share with someone about the 'horrible day I've just had in the office' or to pray for 'my daughter's ear infection' in a relaxed sitting room, rather than a formal pew. The rather unreal 'churchy' language that we use soon gives way to more realistic day-to-day speak that is really healthy in developing 'gritty' love in a fellowship.

And it's when the barriers of formality are broken down in our churches, and we start to see each other as we really are 'warts and all', that we learn to appreciate each other's struggles and long for each other in Christ. Somehow Bible studies become more relevant and alive in home groups. Let's face it, it is so easy to listen to a 40 minute Sunday sermon, and sit back admiring it for its structure and illustration, without ever putting it into action.

But 'chatting' about truth in a small group of Christians who are sitting opposite and all around you, somehow forces you to face up to the practicalities of loving one another in a way that formal church services never do. I'm not so anonymous in my home group. I'm missed when I'm not there. I miss others when they are not there. I am much more aware of the needs of the people in my group, and am more urgent about doing something to meet that need. I feel accountable to the others in my group.

Accountability, however unpopular a word that is in our often easy-come-easy-go environments, is so important in Christian love. God calls us to 'spur one another on towards love and good deeds' (Heb.10:24), to 'not give up meeting together, as some are in the habit of doing', but to 'encourage one another – and all the more as you see the Day (of Christ's return) approaching' (Heb. 10:25). A spur is not comfortable for a horse, but it's the best way of making it move into action. Similarly the intimacy and accountability of 'I-can't-avoid-these-people' home groups, is the best forum to spur each other on in Christ-likeness.

A counter-cultural vision

A friend of mine told me that he once saw a large group enjoying a picnic together in the local park. He knew right away that this strange, diverse grouping from all age ranges and backgrounds 'just had to be a church'. No other group of people in society contains such odds and ends, such an unusual and counter-cultural mix of people – teenagers talking with grandpas, business executives sharing a drink with bricklayers, black and white kicking a ball around. It seemed almost out of place in a park full of young lovers superglued to each others' faces, and senior citizens scowling because a gang of bikers had just roared in.

But that's the glory of God's vision for his church. That strange mixing of peoples from all strata of society, the kind of people who would normally have nothing to do with each other, were actually meeting in a park in Jesus' name. It was just a glimpse of heaven. Who else could this be but the church? What other group of 'peculiar people' have been reconciled to God and to each other. Isn't that a vision worth living for?

Perhaps not everyone at the picnic felt that day was a 'thrill a minute'. Perhaps some of them had to bite their tongues over more edgy remarks that were made in the group. Perhaps others had to strain to take an interest in long-winded conversations with those in the group who were socially awkward. But I know that each one would have learnt something about the church of Jesus Christ. Perhaps a passer-by, who lives a lonely life in a detached house in a loveless world, might look at this strange mix of people sharing a picnic in the park, and inwardly sigh, 'I wish my world could be like that.' That is what church should be.

> By this all men will know that you are my disciples,
> if you love one another (Jn. 13:35).

If we are living our lives as God intends in our church communities, then we will make many passers-by sigh inwardly, 'I wish my world was like that.' God made us to live in community. But community can only really be found in a group of people who are all longing for Christ to be formed in each other. When that happens, Jesus appears, and he even comes and shares a picnic with us in the local park.

A heart that burns for God's people

You cannot engineer a church to be like that. Remember, love is messy. All that you and I can do is deal with our own hearts. Ask yourself today, do I have a loving longing for the people God loves? If Jesus was willing to die for the person I have greatest trouble with in my church, should I not be willing to make an effort? Should I not be willing to be wronged, and take some abuse, even a cold shoulder, just to reach out to them? Is there not something deeply Christ-like about that attitude?

It can be as simple as starting to pray for a person you have problems with. And as you pray it is surprising how the Holy Spirit moves in your soul and starts to give you a godly longing for that person. A longing that is over and above any frustrating traits in their personality.

Is there any way you can change the tone of your relationship with that person? Do they expect a cold glance from you on a Sunday? Could you transform that expectation, and offer a welcoming smile? Why not take time to think about that person's interests? Talk to them about something they delight in. Do a work of kindness for them. Depending on the situation, take them out for a coffee and ask for their forgiveness about the distance there has been in the relationship. Tell them sincerely that you want things to be different. Don't expect any immediate positive moves from them – Jesus had a long time loving us, before there were any moves from us in his direction.

Then if the coldness continues, commit it to the Lord, continue to pray for that person, but be content with the fact that your heart is right towards them. Your longing prayers for them can still make an impact on their lives. But whatever you do, don't throw your hands up in the air and cry 'It's just not worth it!'

Anything that God's heart burns for is eternally worth it. If we had physically watched the agony of the cross, we would have a completely different view of the people on Jesus' heart that day at Calvary. The very best attempts we make – the most sacrificial, humbling moves we make to long for others in Christ's name, are really only scratching the surface of the nail pierced love of Christ.

But, isn't it true that those who love the most, are often the most loved. You cannot ignore for long someone who genuinely desires your spiritual welfare in a loveless world. You cannot hold grudges for long against someone who keeps repaying your spite with blessing and encouragement. Genuine Spirit-filled love breaks down every boundary known to humanity. The love of Christ is the only power that can climb over the barb-wire of the human heart. There is no law that can legislate against love. Love is the very essence of the new human race that God is constructing on the broken body of Jesus.

But more than that, if loving one another really is God's burning desire in the church, then the Spirit himself will make a point of rewarding the efforts we make to long for others in Christ. Unity is his divine calling card. Love is his song. Reproducing the character of Jesus is his passion. If we pursue the most excellent way of love, the Spirit will give wings to our desire.

Review

- God is passionate about his church. We do not think nearly as much of his church as God does. 'Love one another' is the theme song of the burning-heart Christian.
- God has reconciled the church not only to himself but to each other. We cannot have a burning heart if we are only interested in private spirituality, a hermit-like one-to-one relationship with God. We are called to love God in community, and that means striving to love those we might not like humanly speaking.
- Christian love is not a frivolous emotion, it is ultimately a longing for other believers, both at home and in our church, to be like Christ. When people see the church loving in this way, lonely souls will be drawn like a magnet to God's passion for his church.

For personal study

- Think about a time when you experienced the church as God designed it to be – a community where individuals love and serve one another. What made that particular experience so special?
- In what concrete ways can you ensure that your life is less 'detached' from other Christians?
- In practical terms what does it mean to 'long for' other believers in your church?
- Think about the Christians you are closest to – your spouse, other family members and friends – what steps could you take to develop these relationships so that you are 'spurring one another on' in the faith?

Part Four:
Third Chamber: A Heart that Burns for God's World

7

The Longings of God

> O Jerusalem, Jerusalem . . . how often I have longed to gather your children together, as a hen gathers her chicks under her wings, but you were not willing (Mt. 23:37).

The aim of this book is to uncover the deepest passions of God so that as we learn to share these passions with him, our hearts will burn like the Emmaus disciples. So where are the moments in Jesus' life when he is most moved? If we can understand what it was that moved Jesus the most, then surely we are drawing closer to God's most keenly held passions.

It is clear that Jesus did not feel as keenly about every situation he came across. Though Isaiah refers to him as a 'man of sorrows', we should not think of Jesus on the edge of tears every time he faced a sick child or a rebellious crowd. As the perfection of manhood, Jesus was the very essence of balanced emotions. So when we see Jesus' heart unusually moved in moments of high emotion, we need to stop and think about what that means for us. What are the issues of life that ought to move us as people who want to be like Christ and share God's passions?

In Matthew 23 we get an insight into the soul of Jesus. It is a moment of deep emotion when Jesus is wearing his heart on his sleeve. According to Matthew's scheme of events, it is most likely Tuesday of Passion Week. In three days he will be 'lifted up' on a cross outside Jerusalem, above the mocking gaze of jealous religious leaders.

Jesus has just pronounced a long series of 'woes' on the religious leadership of Israel. Woe to the blind guides of Israel, the Pharisees and teachers of the law who reduce God's loving commands to a mechanistic set of regulations. Woe to the hypocrites who promote ritualistic holiness on the outside but whose hearts conceal a cage of snakes. Woe to the religious leaders who have chased and hounded God's people from Abel the first Old Testament martyr, to Zechariah the last.

And then it is as if Jesus is caught up in a moment of instant, heartfelt emotion, like a tearful widow emptying the wardrobe of the husband she has just lost. The fearsome woes pouring out of Jesus against the decadent religion of Israel, suddenly turn into the heartfelt cry of a Saviour longing to gather lost people under his wings.

'O Jerusalem, Jerusalem'. Can you hear it in his voice? 'Out of ignorance you've killed the prophets and you've stoned the righteous men God sent to you for centuries. And in a few days you're going to nail God's own Son to a tree. O Jerusalem, you rebellious, lost child.

> How often I have longed to gather your children together, as a hen gathers her chicks under her wings, but you were not willing (Mt. 23:37).

The Longings of God

What heart-pounding words these are. How is Jesus thinking about this city full of retrograde, hypocritical religious leaders who he knows are scheming to plot his downfall? He thinks of them as little lost chicks running from the protective embrace of a mother hen. 'How often I have longed to gather you . . .' Jesus can peer into the distance and see Roman troops in AD 70 coming to tear apart Jerusalem's temple under God's judgement, and leave the city desolate.

But Jesus' response to this coming judgement is not 'Ha! You got what you deserved!' He grieves for Jerusalem like a father grieves for his lost son. He grieves over their stubborn blindness. If only they could see in him a Saviour, the full expression of God's loving wishes for them. But they were not willing to receive him, so instead they will receive the righteous judgement of God for their rebellion.

Sharing God's love with the lost

It seems to me that this picture of Jesus grieving over Jerusalem is a picture for us as Christians as we consider our response to neighbours, work colleagues, people we bump into at the supermarket. If we are ever to have burning hearts we need to share the passions of God, and God is passionate about lost people. I don't live anywhere near Jerusalem, but I live in another city that God feels deeply for – Aberdeen.

Beneath the veneer of wealth and success that pervades my city, there are little lost chicks running from the embrace of their mother hen. Those might be chicks who prostitute themselves on a Saturday night down some dark alley, or chicks who hate the church and everything it stands for, or simply chicks who are completely ambivalent to God and are heading towards destruction in blissful ignorance. But two things are true of every man and woman in Aberdeen who doesn't know Jesus – they are lost as lost can be, and Jesus longs to gather them under his wings.

A God who longs?

We need to be careful when we talk about a God who longs for lost people. Sometimes I have heard God described as almost a helpless soul, crouched on the end of a cloud in heaven, mourning as he desperately tries to convince people that they need a Saviour. He hopes, he prays, he pleads for people to turn and receive him. But ultimately he becomes the helpless victim of their rejection.

We need to be careful, not because God does not long for lost people, but because there is another side to this coin. God is certainly not helpless. The Bible clearly and repeatedly describes God as the sovereign, almighty ruler of the universe. He sees the beginning from the end. He moves peoples and nations to act under his bidding. In the Old Testament he moved Assyria and Babylon to take his own people into captivity.

God is not the helpless victim of men's decisions. There is a profound mystery here. Paul clearly tells us that one of the reasons we should praise God as believers is because he 'predestined us to be his sons' before the world began. In other words, all those who decide to believe in Christ today, are those whom God has chosen from eternity to be his people. He loved us before we ever loved him. Before we had ever done anything right or wrong, God had chosen us to be part of his family to the praise of his glory.

Salvation is ultimately the work of God. To deny that, simply because it is hard to understand, is to play around with powerful, repeated truths in Scripture until we feel comfortable about God. When Paul discusses the issue of God choosing some and not others for salvation in Romans 9 to 11, he ends up with a song of praise to God because God's ways are so much higher than ours, and his plans so much wiser.

How unsearchable his judgments, and his paths beyond tracing out! (Rom. 11:33).

When Paul describes God's plan of salvation as 'unsearchable' and 'beyond tracing out', surely we have to pause for a moment. There comes a point when God's choices and decisions, his breathtaking mastery over every happening in the history of the world, is just beyond our finite, sinful minds to understand. If God says that he is just and righteous in every decision he makes, and the Scriptures are loaded with that affirmation, then we must reach out in faith and say 'Lord, I don't understand your ways, but I trust you.
'I cannot fathom how you move men's hearts. I have little ultimate understanding of how you will judge the soul of each man and woman, or how you are moving world history on to its glorious conclusion when Christ will return and your church will be gathered to you. I cannot understand what it means to be God. What it must be like to have your fathomless mind, your profound, eternal understanding. But like a young child lying in the lap of his father, I trust you. I know you are good, that your love endures forever. And I will rest in that.'

I have found that Psalm 131 is helpful to pray through when I come across mysteries in Scripture I cannot fathom. This is a prayer of David, King of Israel who, despite his own greatness and throne, lies in the lap of his heavenly father and trusts him for things he does not understand.

> I do not concern myself with great matters
> or things too wonderful for me.
> But I have stilled and quietened my soul;
> like a weaned child with its mother,
> like a weaned child is my soul within me
> (Ps. 131:1,2)

So when we think about God longing for lost people, we must not think of a doting, helpless daddy hoping against hope that people decide for him. Rather he is the Sovereign Father, the 'alpha and omega' of salvation. He has already seen the day when his ransomed people will be gathered into the glories of heaven with him, as well as the day when he will command his angels to open the Lake of Fire. And yet he is a Sovereign Lord who longs to gather lost people under his wings. He grieves that they will not enter his warm embrace.

Do we long?

What troubles me is that many Christians have so emphasized the sovereignty of God that they have argued themselves out of longing for lost people the way God clearly does. There are Christians who are entangled in discussions about whether Jesus really did die for all people, or only for God's chosen people, that God's passion for lost people becomes secondary to theological arguments.

The Longings of God

Sometimes preachers get so caught up with the fact that God chooses people from eternity, that they have lost all persuasiveness from their preaching. When they talk to unbelievers, it does not sound like they are longing for them to find Christ. In a strange way their reading of Scripture prevents them from truly sharing God's heart for the lost.

And yet this desire for lost people to be saved is at the heart of some of the deepest emotions in Scripture. I can almost see Jesus with his hands outstretched as he beckons to people

> Come to me, all you who are weary and burdened and I will give you rest (Mt. 11:28).

I can feel Paul's zeal as he wishes that he could give up his own salvation so that his Jewish brothers and sisters, whom he prays and longs for, might discover Christ.

> I have great sorrow and unceasing anguish in my heart. For I could wish that I myself were cursed and cut off from Christ for the sake of my brothers, those of my own race, the people of Israel (Rom. 9:2-4a).

What a thing to say. Especially from the man who has got closer than most to appreciating the full wonder of God's salvation. That he could even entertain the thought of losing his salvation and face hell, so that his fellow Israelites might take his place in heaven. What a challenge for us about the way we should look at the unbelievers in our community whom God has sovereignly placed in our lives.

A heart that burns for all lost people

However we understand God's sovereign control over salvation, it is clear from the Bible that we cannot share his passions until our hearts burn without compromise, for all the people in this world who do not know him personally. God has not told us which of our neighbours or work colleagues are 'elect', and which are not. Paul knew that the vast majority of Jews in his day, to whom he preached the gospel as a first priority (Rom. 1:17), were going to reject his message, and indeed were being hardened by God (Rom. 9 – 11).

But that did not stop him longing for them, preaching persuasively to them, or praying specifically for them. At no stage did he try to identify which Jews God was choosing, and which he was rejecting. He longed for them all with unceasing anguish. He prayed earnestly for their salvation, while leaving all ultimate judgements in God's infinitely wiser hands.

In fact Paul, the apostle who spoke more about divine election that any other, also pours out his passion for lost people more than any other Bible writer. He writes to the Corinthians with intense emotion that comes from his burning heart.

> I make myself a slave to everyone, to win as many as possible . . . I have become all things to all men so that by all possible means I might save some (1 Cor. 9:19,22).

What a tragedy it is when we try to remove the mystery of God's sovereignty in salvation and his passion for lost people, and end up with a cold, calculating gospel. However compelling the 'election' passages are in the

The Longings of God

Bible, we cannot read the Scriptures with 'tunnel vision'. To underplay God's longing passion for lost people from the sacred pages of Scripture is to compromise some of God's deepest emotions.

God is like a father looking outside the window of his house daily, waiting for his prodigal children to return (Luke 15). Jesus weeps, 'O Jerusalem, Jerusalem... how I long to gather you... Come to me, all you who are weary' (See Lk. 13:34; Mt. 11:28). We should not let our understanding of other Scriptures empty these clearly divine emotions of their power.

Motivations to witness

Let me share with you an issue I have struggled with when it comes to longing for lost people. I have heard many well-intentioned speakers try to persuade believers to be more active in personal evangelism. Quite often in an emotional appeal, they will paint foreboding pictures of the fires of hell, and then ask us if we feel nothing about people who are heading to a lost eternity.

I have preached that way occasionally myself and without doubt, the thought of the horrors of hell is a powerful incentive to share the gospel. Indeed to cast doubts over the reality of hell, as some Christians are doing today, is to play around with fundamental Christian doctrine, and presents a danger to the truth, on a par with putting Christ's body back in the empty tomb.

Over the years, however, it has struck me how seldom the Bible uses hell as a motivation for evangelism. It paints clear, uncompromising pictures of hell and frequently challenges us about our need to witness for Christ. But hell is rarely used as an incentive to witness in the Bible.

So what incentives does the Bible give for us as Christians to witness? It seems to me that if hell is our only reason for witness, we run the risk of getting angry with God, who invented hell, for not saving more people, and reduces our witnessing to a more desperate, guilt-driven desire than it ought to be. But did you realize that witnessing is part of our worship to God?

Hebrews 13 speaks about witnessing in a clear worship context.

> Through Jesus, therefore, let us continually offer to God a sacrifice of praise – the fruit of lips that confess his name (Heb. 13:15)

In other words, part of our 'sacrifice of praise' as Christians, is to have lips that publicly confess the name of Jesus. This verse is in the context of Christians being willing to stand out for their faith in a godless world, and face the shame that Jesus faced. When we stand out as Christians who publicly confess the name of Jesus, and face the ridicule that may well result, we are worshipping God. What a beautiful, highly motivating reason to witness.

But more than this, the biggest motivation the Bible gives to witness, is the glory of God. God wants us to long with him for that day when believers from 'every nation, tribe, people and language' (Rev. 7:9) will gather in front of his throne and worship him forever. That is the incentive that stirs our burning hearts – to get people ready for the day when they will stand in front of King Jesus, and praise the Saviour who died for them.

Hebrews tells us that Jesus endured the agony of the cross 'for the joy that was set before him'. How on earth could Jesus have had any joy in the shameful cross?

Precisely this – the joy that drove him to the cross, was the thought that God would use his cross to call people from every nation in the world to be his children, and share eternity with him to the praise of his glory. When that heavenly gathering becomes my incentive for witnessing for Christ, when I begin to see my witness as my 'sacrifice of praise', then witnessing becomes less guilt-driven, and more worship inspired. I witness because I share the same heartbeat that drove Christ to the cross.

None of this is to say that the reality of hell is not a valid motive for witnessing. God does not delight in the death of the wicked. He wants people to be rescued from hell (see the similar 'that none may perish' desires in John 3:16 and 2 Peter 3:9). But if hell is my *only* motivation for speaking about Christ, then I might lose the joy of witnessing, the burning heart to witness that stems from my wish to please Christ and see him glorified in front of the countless multitudes of his redeemed children. Heaven is a vision to inspire. Heaven is a dream to live for. These pure, Christ-centred motives cannot be conjured up in an instant. They are the process of a life spent growing in our knowledge and enjoyment of God. We need to pray that God by his Spirit would gradually fill us with these desires, so that witnessing becomes for us the joy it ought to be, and not a guilt induced trial we shrivel away from.

8

Reaching Out with God's Love

If our hearts are to burn for God's world we need to be moved by the lost chicks in our immediate environment. We need to be moved, not just by a vision of angels casting these souls into everlasting darkness – we need a fresh vision of that majestic chorus of men and women from every nation bringing their praise into the heavenly city.

If we could learn to see worship not just as heartfelt singing on a Sunday, but confessing Jesus' name to lost chicks on a Monday, our hearts might just begin to burn. These desires are not instinctive desires. They are given to us by the Holy Spirit who inspires in us the passions of God. But like music lovers who long for a concert, and sport lovers who long for the big game, we need to be God lovers who long for a lost world to be remade in the image of its creator.

If you have been praying for a growing desire in your heart to see lost people won for Christ, and it's just not happening – your spirit is just not moved by the needs of neighbours – then please do not think you are some kind of lost cause. A longing for lost people is a desire that the Holy Spirit cultivates over a long period of time.

The problem often is that the people we are praying for remain a bland, faceless multitude. I find it very difficult to pray longingly for people to find Christ when I know very little about them. The very best way to develop a longing heart for lost people is to be intentional about building relationships with them. People are much more likely to truly grab our hearts when we get to know the issues they are struggling with – even when we have a chance to see their spiritual blindness up close. Pity for another lost person is powerfully provocative and biblical. Jesus longed for Israelites who were 'like sheep without a shepherd' (Mt. 9:36).

Building evangelistic relationships

God will not give us a burning heart for lost people as we sit in our closets and pray for them. That is not to demean the power of prayer in any way, but if God is to see that our prayers are truly heartfelt, then surely he needs to see us doing our best to make contact with this faceless world we are praying for.

The cause of evangelism has so often been blunted by well-meaning Christians who limit evangelism to forcing a gospel tract into the hands of people they have never spoken to. Please don't misunderstand – giving out gospel literature is much better than nothing. It allows us to deliver a compact presentation of Christian truth to people who might never have heard it before. God can certainly use that kind of witnessing powerfully, and I know there are many illuminating stories of how he has done just that.

But let us be in no doubt – a tract swiftly placed under a car windscreen, or through a local letterbox cannot compare with the power of a caring Christian developing a bond with an unbeliever in his natural sphere of influence. If you asked at your local church this Sunday for people to put their hands up if they were saved through a tract or a relationship, I would be massively surprised if the vast majority did not have in their minds the person who first introduced them to Jesus.

Building natural relationships with unbelievers has always been and will always be the most powerful method of introducing lost chicks to their Saviour. And I emphasize the term 'natural relationships'. We don't need to wait for a one-off conversation with the person we sit next to on the bus or train for an evangelistic opportunity. Though there are often openings to share about our faith with our hairdresser, the lady who serves us regularly at the local chip shop, even the man who swipes our credit card at the filling station, these are probably not the most 'natural relationships' in our lives.

Our most natural relationships are people we see the most often, not because we plan to see them, but because our lives are interconnected in some way that allows us time to influence and understand them. The most glaring examples of that are family, immediate neighbours, and perhaps most compellingly our work colleagues.

Seeing our workplace as a mission field

Probably the least tapped mission field operates from nine to five (or increasingly 'eight till late') every day. I was rather embarrassed as a pastor and regular preacher to read an article recently about the lack of time the church devotes to preparing people for evangelism in the workplace. Alistair Mackenzie, a New Zealander, in an article produced for *Canvas* magazine stated that most Christians spend 40 per cent of their waking hours at work and only 2 per cent at church. And yet I'm sure we would agree with Mackenzie's conclusion that we put most of our energy into that 2 per cent of time rather than that 40 per cent of time.

For all sorts of reasons, the world of work offers the most compelling mission field to every Christian worker. Apart from unusual working scenarios, work is the place where we are most constantly surrounded by unbelievers. Our lives are automatically interconnected with them in relationally significant ways. We are put in teams with them, whether they like that or not. They rub shoulders with us out of necessity every working day.

I smile sometimes at the joy Paul receives in his prison cell in Philippians 1, chained every moment of every day to a member of Caesar's elite praetorian guard. Paul sees this as a wonderful opportunity for the gospel as the guard is not allowed to leave Paul's side, and has to hear Paul's glorious Damascus Road testimony. I cannot imagine a single guard leaving Paul's cell without having heard the Christ story (cf. Phil. 1:12,13). It seems that Christ is being talked about among Caesar's most elite troops as Paul awaits his sentence.

How similar that is to the situation we often find ourselves in at work, with unbelievers who must work closely alongside us, hear the way we speak, and note the way we act under pressure. We cannot help but allow our character and testimony to be seen and heard. And yet how seldom we view our work as the place we do our best ministry.

Workplace blues

I remember my first few days in the workplace. It was a secondary school staffroom outside Durham. In my naïve youthfulness, I had been excited by the opportunity of bringing revival to a local school with fellow teachers falling on their knees in repentance. What I discovered was a group of older teachers smoking in the corner, grumbling about how much teaching had changed, and how little control they had in the classroom. Anyone who wanted to bring any kind of positive note into the scenario was quickly made an outcast. Frankly, the staffroom made me run for cover back to my comfortable church Bible studies.

I would imagine that many Christians have a similar experience. They are dragged into the same negativity about work as their workmates around them. Any excitement that the working environment could be a powerful mission field soon dissolves. As Christians we can so easily get dragged into the 'rat race'. We can find ourselves influenced by the negative culture at work rather than influencing it.

We have the same career and moneymaking aspirations as the next man. We are laid low by the same pressures, and when we add our church commitments (which our colleagues don't face) to our increasingly demanding work commitments, a burning heart for mission is soon drowned out by the pressures of squeezing several different lives into one.

'Be transformed by the renewing of your minds'

And yet we should not settle for that. God calls us as Christians to be constantly renewing our mindsets (Rom.

12:2) – seeing all of life through the lens of our relationship with Christ, and that includes our workplace. It is possible to be a dynamic witness for Christ, *because* of the negative atmosphere at work rather than despite it. What a difference a godly man or woman can have in a dark setting – the light shines all the more brightly (Phil. 1:12-14).

Bringing Jesus to work begins with looking at the value of your work through his redeeming eyes. Too many Christians force an anti-biblical distinction between 'secular' work and 'spiritual' work. The thinking goes like this – those who are doing the really important work for God are the pastors and worship leaders at church. That's spiritual work. My 'secular' work by comparison is bland, dull and pointless. It is so driven by the 'bottom line' in my company, or by bosses who want to climb the career ladder, that God is nowhere in sight.

I've simply got to get through my job as honestly as I can, and then try and squeeze some properly 'spiritual' work in at church to make my life worthwhile for Jesus. This kind of thinking has devastated workplace evangelism, but is often reinforced by churches who praise their Sunday school teachers, but never highlight the profoundly spiritual work of, say, a Christian nurse on the wards.

The Bible's view of work is altogether different. God made us to be workers. In fact the very first thing God does in the Bible is work – he creates in Genesis 1. And the very first thing God asks man to do is work. He places him in the garden and tells him to subdue creation around him – Adam wasn't called to be a priest, God called him to be a gardener. And everything about that original creation was good and pleasing to God. In fact the Bible repeatedly states the 'glory' of work. It is part of us bearing God's image. Psalm 8 declares

> You made him (humanity) a little lower than the heavenly beings and crowned him with glory and honour. You made him ruler over the works of your hands; you put everything under his feet (Ps. 8:5,6).

Our work is the sign of our dominion over God's creation. The Christian accountant who looks after peoples' finances is helping the world run smoothly just as much as Adam tilling the soil. The Christian lawyer hearing and defending cases can bring God's justice to the world, and it is pleasing to the Lord. This distinction between 'secular' and 'spiritual' work is a false one that needs to be roundly rejected if we as believers are to have burning hearts for Christ at work.

Jesus transforms even menial work

The New Testament provides great encouragement for workers who find themselves doing the most menial of tasks either on the factory floor, or even doing the dishes. Ephesians 6 compares Christians obeying their earthly bosses to

> doing the will of God from your heart (Eph. 6:6).

Such lofty language is not reserved for the Billy Grahams of our world, but for Christian car mechanics, bricklayers, dentists, librarians, you name it. In fact Paul transforms every menial task in our lives into a potential act of worship launched to God from a burning heart

> ... whatever you do, do it all for the glory of God (1 Cor. 10:31).

What a profound impact we could make for Christ in our workplace if we saw our work as truly 'spiritual'. We would work with absolute devotion because it is part of our glory as creations of a working God. We would approach every menial task as an opportunity to bring glory to God in our attitudes and take these attitudes with us into every situation – grand and glorious, or apparently trivial and meaningless. All can be worship.

If we could bring this kind of purpose and passion into our working lives, we would certainly stand out for Christ, and be a means of pointing lost and empty chicks towards a new way of living.

But perhaps the most significant way we can witness at work is by bringing the kind of pastoral care ethos we so often hear about at church into our offices and factory floors.

Evangelistic pastoral care

In almost every area of employment today, we have become a 'target driven' culture. So many workplaces revolve around hitting the targets set for us at the beginning of the year. Those working in big companies driven by such targets may find themselves viewed purely in terms of their productivity rather than as individuals. You are unlikely to be asked in your annual review, 'How are your children doing? How well has your mum recovered from her hip operation?'

Companies exchange genuine care for their employees for good wages and company 'perks'. That is not the same as showing concern for your workforce. Generous salaries do not make for emotionally well-adjusted human beings. In fact they quite often promote the 'judge-people-according-to-their-productivity' principle that is so damaging to the human personality.

Here is an area where Christians can be 'salt and light' (Mt. 5:13-16), promoting people in an environment that is so productivity based. Look out for the loners in your office or staffroom. Have you ever asked them about their families, their health, their life outside work? Loners in the workplace are probably people who are reeling from the coldness and distancing created by 'bottom line' driven businesses.

What a difference a Christian can make who is genuinely interested in the whole person, who asks the kind of 'heart and soul' questions no one else asks or is interested in. Casual conversations in the workplace, which we often use just to fill the time in a monotonous day, can be powerful evangelistic opportunities.

That person who cleans out your office, or whom you find smoking alone in some dark corner over lunch – he or she is a lost chick, a potential divine appointment if we only had eyes to see. Colossians 4:5,6 are great words to read every day before going to work

> Be wise in the way you act towards outsiders; make the most of every opportunity. Let your conversation be always full of grace, seasoned with salt, so that you may know how to answer everyone.

Genuinely caring Christians, who consistently show a rounded interest in the lives of their working colleagues, quickly make a reputation for themselves at work. When a secretary has suffered a bereavement in their family – her mother has just died, or a brother or sister is involved in a car crash – who are they going to turn to for emotional support during that time of crisis? People in that kind of emotional trauma don't necessarily confide in their mates with whom they go 'clubbing' on a Friday night. But it is amazing how often they will pour out their heart to the Christian who really cares.

That Christian and that 'worldly' secretary may have nothing else in common. They may never have had a single social moment together outside the office. But when human tragedy strikes, and a lost chick is crying out for the kind of agape love they cannot find among other work colleagues, a caring Christian can be an open door to the Kingdom of God. Genuine, Christ-like love can be shared in some of the most unlikely places, when a Christian transforms their work by placing people ahead of productivity.

Mark Greene, who works for the London Institute for Contemporary Christianity, constantly challenges Christians to see the opportunities of workplace evangelism. In his excellent book *Thank God it's Monday* (Milton Keynes: Scripture Union, 1997) Greene bemoans the fact that church so often emphasizes witnessing to the community around us, developing relationships with our next door neighbours, when all the time a vast untapped sea of evangelistic opportunities is waiting for us at work, if we will only open our eyes.

> Church calls on us to build bridges with our neighbours, to look for common ground with people in our community. We are encouraged to fish in pools and puddles, when we are sitting on a lake full of fish.

May we see with fresh eyes the 'lake full of fish' that Jesus is calling us to catch in his name.

9

A Desire for All Nations

A subject that is increasingly neglected today when it comes to longing for lost people to know Christ, is the theme of world mission. It is a good sign that a Christian is growing in their maturity when they begin to grow in passion, not just for family members and neighbours to know Christ, but for nations across the world to be reached. World mission is not some obscure theme hidden away in mysterious books like Zephaniah. The Bible pulsates with God's world vision.

Right from the moment God called Abraham to leave his country and go to a place God would show him, God's heart has always burned for the world as a whole. Through Abraham, God would establish Israel as his chosen people, a holy nation, so that they could bring the love of God to the entire globe. God's vision for world mission appears as early as Genesis 12 where God promises Abraham

> all peoples on earth will be blessed through you (Gen. 12:3).

The fact that Israel became a very inward-looking culture that despised the surrounding nations, did not reflect God's heart to reach people across the globe. Israel failed in its God-given task to be a light to the world. The book of Jonah shows just how insular Israel had become, despising the foreign pagans from surrounding countries, rather than showing them the truth of God. Jonah is a hard-hitting book that is in the Bible to highlight our own prejudices against lost people. We can see our own hearts in the negative example of Jonah the prophet, who is smug about his own holiness, and hates the mercy God extends to pagan foreigners.

The world's worst missionary

Jonah is 'Mr Arrogant', who struts around parading his 'God's own people' Jewishness. Initially he runs from God's call to preach to pagan Nineveh. His reason for running is not because he lacks courage as a preacher. He runs because he knows that God is

> gracious and compassionate . . . slow to anger and abounding in love (Jon. 4:2).

He thinks to himself, 'If I preach to these despicable Ninevites, I know exactly what God's going to do. He's going to go and forgive them, isn't he. He's going to let those abusive, foul-mouthed idol worshippers in on his grace. I can't stomach that!' So Jonah makes a run for it, and plunges straight into the gastric juices of a great fish.

In his so-called prayer of repentance from inside the great fish, his arrogance is clear. He uses the self-centred pronoun 'I' ten times in his nine verse prayer (Jon. 2), and closes with his disdain for the Ninevites

> Those who cling to worthless idols forfeit the grace that could be theirs. But I . . . will sacrifice to you. What I have vowed I will make good (Jon. 2:8,9).

'Lord, you can never trust heathen scum like the Ninevites. You can only depend on righteous prophets like me!' Intriguingly the great fish literally 'vomits' Jonah up (Jon. 2:10). Is Jonah's lack of missionary zeal sickening to God like the 'lukewarm' Christianity of the church in Laodicea (Rev. 3:16)?

When Jonah finally preaches to Nineveh, the whole city is cut to the heart and repents in the kind of revival barely seen among God's own people. And what does Jonah do? Is he on his knees praising God for his grace, as he has now become the most 'successful' prophet in the Old Testament (Isaiah and Jeremiah would not have minded Jonah's assignment)?

No! Jonah is seething at God's mercy. The thought of these pagan foreigners revelling in God's forgiveness made Jonah want to commit suicide. As he sits outside the city in despair, hoping that fire will fall from heaven on Nineveh he cries

> Now, O Lord, take away my life, for it is better for me to die than to live (Jon. 4:3).

Why is this hypocritical prophet in the Bible, we ask? He's there to show us God's burning heart for the globe – that he should desire to save a pagan, godless city like Nineveh – and to challenge his people down the ages who are so comfortable with their 'God's own people' status that they have no heart for the nations. As Jonah sits in the noonday sun, waiting for God to judge the pagan foreigners, God causes a vine to grow and provide shade for him.

Jonah is 'very happy' about the vine (Jon. 4:6). He loves it when God is looking after his personal comforts, showing him mercy that he doesn't deserve as a rebellious prophet. And yet Jonah begrudges that same mercy being shown by God to ignorant pagan cities like Nineveh. Jonah is the only book in the Bible that closes with a question, so the question must be important. It is a question that uncovers God's burning heart for foreign nations.

> Nineveh has more than a hundred and twenty thousand people who cannot tell their right hand from their left . . . Should I not be concerned about that great city? (Jon. 4:11)

The answer to God's question is of course 'yes'. God should be concerned about the godless city of Nineveh. But more to the point, so should Jonah, God's self-centred prophet. He revels in the mercy that has been shown him, but hates it when God shows that mercy to undeserving foreigners. And so should we, if we want to have a burning heart.

God looks at sprawling cities like Calcutta, Manila, Beijing, Rio, Kabul, Istanbul, places where, spiritually speaking, the people cannot tell their right hand from the left. Many of these cities are surrounded by Buddhist temples and shrines, Islamic mosques, and some simply crushed under the weight of secularism and an atheistic state. We need to look at them through God's burning heart and ask, 'Should I not be concerned about that great city?'

Where have all the missionaries gone?

Interest in world mission is fading. Ironically in a day when we live in a 'global village', and our advanced transport systems can get us relatively cheaply to almost any part of the world within a couple of days, no one is going.

When you ask even committed young people in the 'twenty-something' age bracket in our churches 'would you be interested in world mission?' they don't really know what you are talking about. The average evangelical church may send a couple of young people on a two-week summer mission, but the concept of committing to long-term mission is becoming increasingly rare.

When young people are looking at career possibilities as they fill out their forms for universities and work experience, pastoring a church and/or mission work are rarely even on the radar. It is not the fault of the young people. World mission gets little time in our pulpits. Often world mission gets 'delegated' to a missions' committee that meets twice a year to discuss how soon the patchwork quilts that were put together lovingly by the 'women's guild' can be sent to the pastor's second cousin in 'Mowzambeeke'. Should we not be more concerned for the world's great cities? Should more of us not be encouraged to leave our jobs and set off on a reckless journey of faith and die gloriously on some foreign mission field? Instead of writing on our tombstone 'He moved from lower to upper management in the waterproof coat department of Marks and Spencer', they could honestly write, 'He gave himself to God's global vision of reaching the nations for Christ'.

Getting world mission on the agenda

We need to rediscover God's passion for world mission, and drag it kicking and screaming to the forefront of our minds. Do you have the date and time on a calendar somewhere in your home when God told you that you were definitely *not* called to the mission field, having given the thought full consideration, and told him you were willing to go anywhere at any time?

For every Christian to seriously consider going on the mission field is an uncomfortable challenge. But God's burning heart for mission across the globe is undiminished since the day he called Abraham to leave his own country, and promised that his children would be a blessing across the nations. We are those children.

It is telling that the call of Abraham in Genesis 12 immediately follows God's judgement on the nations at the Tower of Babel in Genesis 11, scattering them across the globe, and confusing them with different languages. The passion behind world mission is to reverse the effects of Babel's curse, and to call the nations together again under the banner of the cross. One day all nations will sing a new song to Christ, in a common language, before the throne of God

> You are worthy to take the scroll... because you were slain, and with your blood you purchased men for God from every tribe and language and people and nation. You have made them to be a kingdom and priests to serve our God, and they will reign on the earth (Rev. 5:9,10).

If world mission is a theme that spreads from Genesis to Revelation; if the book of Jonah was specifically written to rebuke Christians for a lack of concern for God's great foreign cities; if world mission was at the heart of the manifesto that Jesus left for his disciples – 'Go into all the world' (see Mt. 28:19) – a task they could not have possibly accomplished in their own generation; if one of the 'signs' that will precede the coming again of Christ is that the gospel will spread to the four corners of the earth (Mt. 24:14); if the whole goal of redemption is for a multicoloured, multi-ethnic rainbow of worship to vibrate in heaven for all eternity, *then* surely God must have a burning heart for world mission. And, if we are to share God's passions, and hold at bay the apathy that our dying local churches may drive us to, then we should have a burning heart for world mission too.

Opening our eyes to God's global vision

So how can we open your eyes to the wider world, and start to feel God's missionary zeal? Again our greatest problem when it comes to passion for the lost world, is staring out into a faceless multitude.

Praying passionately for the people of Burma tonight is going to be a real struggle if I know no one who is Burmese, and have no understanding of the needs of Burmese missionaries. But there is help at hand. Patrick Johnstone's best-selling book *Operation World* (Milton Keynes: Authentic Lifestyle, 2001, Revised 2005) is a veritable treasure trove of valuable information on mission needs across the globe, country by country. Why not start reading about Burma, or Qatar, or the state of the church in Iraq? Johnstone's book is great to pick up even for five minutes at a time.

As you read about a country a day, you begin to sense God's burning heart for the nations, and enter into the aspirations of generations of men and women who left their homeland with nothing but their faith, and became ambassadors for Christ to the nations: Hudson Taylor, William Carey, Gladys Aylward, David Livingstone, Eric Liddle, Jim Elliot, David Brainerd, Henry Martyn. Generations of men and women who have no enduring city to call their own in this world. Pilgrims who were 'looking forward to the city with foundations, whose architect and builder is God' (Heb. 11:10).

As the Hebrew writer would say about these great heroes of faith

the world was not worthy of them (Heb. 11:38).

What if we were to catch that same pilgrim vision for the nations today? What if we could be known as those of whom the world is not worthy?

Getting in touch with missionaries

One of the best ways to develop a heart for world mission, is by getting in touch with one of the missionaries your church supports. Missionaries, who have been displaced from their familiar culture and find themselves trying to preach Jesus in a completely alien environment, welcome any contact they can have with 'home'.

I remember when I was in Spain for a year, I loved receiving something as simple as newspaper clippings from the *Daily Mail*, sports results, and regular news of what was going on in my 'home' church. Even the most basic elements of home culture that we take for granted can be a heart-warming gift to a missionary on the field. I know missionaries who would love nothing better than a can of baked beans, a jar of peanut butter – even the perversity of a jar of Marmite, because they can't get these 'tastes of home' where they live.

Email one of your missionaries, find out what they would like sent out, and even get a team together to provide it. What struggles are they facing with the language and the culture? How are their children adapting to foreign schooling? What are the church issues they are dealing with? Who are the people they are praying for to come to Christ?

It can really 'spice up' you prayer life when you start praying for 'Luigi', an Argentinian drug addict who came to an outreach evening at the church of one of 'your missionaries'. This kind of commitment helps you play a part in God's goal of spreading his glory around the globe, it will mature your prayer life, and will encourage missionaries who often feel abandoned by the churches who commissioned them to their work.

Who knows what that kind of contact can lead to? I know of several Christians who made this kind of commitment to missionaries early in their life while they were in regular employment. Later they either lost their job or took early retirement, and ended up working with those same missionaries in Brazil and Korea and Surinam. Suddenly a whole life that could have ended in deep frustration at lost employment, or worse still, could have been frittered away, ended with a burning heart being poured out in the great passion of bringing the nations to God.

May God teach us not to live small, safe, routine lives, but to lift our eyes, even in little ways, to the needs of the world he loves. God's call to world mission should be

A Desire for All Nations

gathering momentum in our hearts, in the 'global village' in which we live. The day of his appearing is getting closer.

Review

- God is passionate about his world. Some of Christ's deepest emotions when he was on earth related to his desire to see lost, rebellious people come back to the Father who loves them.
- Whatever our views on divine election, and election is clearly taught in Scripture, we cannot edit God's passionate longing for lost people from the pages of his Word. If we do, we end up with a calculating rather than a passionate gospel.
- Burning-heart believers look on their friends, neighbours, working colleagues and unbelieving family as lost chicks whom Christ is longing to draw to himself.
- God is also passionate for the nations, the great cities of our world. Burning-heart believers are those who are learning to lift their eyes from their immediate surroundings, and share God's world vision by joining in missionary enterprise.

For personal study

- In what ways can our view of God's sovereignty impact our desire to witness? How has your reading of the Bible shaped your attitude to unbelievers around you?
- What has been your past experience of witnessing – consider your fears, struggles, and moments of greatest elation. How can we improve our attitude to

witnessing seeing it less as a 'guilt induced trial', and more of a 'joy'?
- Think about your work situation (this involves paid employment, managing the home, voluntary work etc.). How can you influence your work situation and the people in it for Christ? What attitudes do you need to change? What action do you need to take?
- What practical steps can you take to share God's heart for the nations, and increase your commitment to world mission?

Part Five:
Fourth Chamber: A Heart that Burns for God's Return

10

Jesus is Coming Again

> Keep watch, because you do not know on what day your Lord will come (Mt. 24:42).

As I look out of my office window this morning, there is nothing but the faintest breeze in the air. Leaves on the trees that adorn my view are limp. The Deeside hills in the background look as sturdy and fixed as the day God formed them at the dawn of creation. The only sound that invades the peace of this scene is the occasional passing car. It is hard to imagine on a day like today, that Jesus is coming back again, and we are heading for a cosmic meltdown.

But any serious reader of the Bible cannot escape the conclusion that God's story still awaits its final chapter. What has been set in motion through the cross, and the invasion of Satan's territory by the Kingdom of God, is crying out for a conclusion.

The people of God, being gathered from every nation under the banner of Christ's blood, still live in a world that is under God's curse (Gen. 3). We await the consummation. Our aching limbs long to be clothed with immortality. Our aching souls, all too aware of our ongoing failings, long to be perfect like Christ. Even the world around us, the physical creation itself, abused by industrialists and pollution, is groaning for the One who will establish a 'new heavens and a new earth, the home of righteousness'.

There is something missing from our burning hearts if we are longing for God's glory (first chamber), pining for God's people (second chamber), witnessing to God's world (third chamber), but are not yearning for the day Jesus will come to reign (fourth chamber).

An enormous amount of intrigue and speculation has surrounded this heart-pounding thought of the return of Christ. The purpose of this chapter is not to rehash views on millenniums, tribulations, beasts with ten heads, or who I think Antichrist might be (my former physics teacher is probably too old to make a serious impact on world history now, so is out of the running!). In any case, the endless speculation about the 'last times' often hides the most important truths that we need to know about the issue. Jesus will come unexpectedly. We should be longing for his coming. And we need to be ready to meet him. These are the issues that will dominate this chapter.

The return of Christ is fundamental

The return of Christ to the earth is as fundamental to Christianity as the cross and the resurrection. Some liberal theologians may have placed doubts on the nature of his coming, suggesting that it is more a mystical spiritual experience, than a physical reality. However, the New Testament is categorical that Jesus will return to the earth on some future day in real 'space and time'.

Jesus is Coming Again

He will come back *visibly*. That is the clear implication of the message of the angels at the beginning of the book of Acts. In fact it is the message of the angels convincing the disciples that Jesus will come again, that is the introduction to all the urgent public witness of the church throughout the book. While the disciples are standing on the mountain with open mouths, seeing Jesus' resurrected body literally disappear from view behind the clouds, 'suddenly two men dressed in white' appear beside them (Acts 1:10).

The message of the angels is difficult to misinterpret.

> Why do you stand here looking into the sky? This same Jesus, who has been taken from you into heaven, will come back in the same way you have seen him go into heaven (Acts 1:10,11).

This verse is not just saying that Jesus is coming back again. It is saying that he will come back again *in the same way* he left our world 2,000 years ago. He will be seen coming through the clouds in the sky. His glorious return has no mysticism about it. Luke is clearly not saying that Jesus' return will just be an intangible spiritual experience. Jesus' return will be visible and literal, a real historical event. Not that we needed Acts to tell us that. Jesus had already spelt it out several times in the Gospels, even when he was under the most intense pressure at his trial.

> In the future you will see the Son of Man sitting at the right hand of the Mighty One and coming on the clouds of heaven (Mt. 26:64).

Again the emphasis is on 'you will see'. Jesus' second coming will not be some hidden, private event like his first coming that was shared with just a handful of shepherds and some eastern astrologers. His second coming will be the most visible, public event that God has ever unleashed before humanity's eyes in the history of the world. No one saw God create the world. But every eye will see the glorious return of Christ. Matthew 24 suggests that all the nations of the earth will be caught up with his coming.

> At that time the sign of the Son of Man will appear in the sky, and all the nations of the earth will mourn. They will see the Son of Man coming on the clouds of the sky, with power and great glory (Mt. 24:30).

God wants the whole world to see the coming of Christ, because that will be the full unveiling of Christ's 'glory and power'. The 'hiddenness' of God's Kingdom will be removed forever. All people will see Jesus for who he truly is. In our day of advanced satellite systems and Internet technology, it is possible like never before, for the whole earth to see Jesus coming in the clouds of heaven, at the same time.

Jesus will return suddenly

Jesus will not only appear *visibly*, he will also return *suddenly*. While there will be certain signs that will point to his coming (wars and rumours of wars, earthquakes, famines, the worldwide spread of the gospel and so on in Matthew 24), basically Jesus' coming will catch everyone by surprise. Paul points to the kind of atmosphere that will pervade peoples' minds on the day Christ comes.

> The day of the Lord will come like a thief in the night. While people are saying 'Peace and safety', destruction will come on them suddenly, as labour pains on a pregnant woman, and they will not escape (1 Thes. 5:2,3).

It is an atmosphere of 'peace and safety' that will be filling peoples' hearts when Jesus comes again. They will not be expecting it. Matthew compares the suddenness of Jesus' coming to the day when God closed the door of the ark, before the flood literally swept people off their feet. In Noah's day, life was very much continuing as usual. Yes, there were warnings from the crazy old man who was building the mother of all boats when there had been no rain for months, but other than that people were

> eating and drinking, marrying and giving in marriage, up to the day Noah entered the ark (Mt. 24:38).

Life was continuing as normal. Just like the view from my office this morning, all was 'peace' and 'safety'. And then in an instant, cosmic calamity. The destruction of every living creature on the face of the earth, apart from those who were safe inside the wooden boat that God had prepared for their salvation.

As I sit here today there are soldiers in Iraq. An earthquake has recently caused tsunami waves to devastate South East Asia, and a hurricane in the States has brought a superpower to its knees. Despite how normal everything looks from my office, many of the 'signs' of Jesus' coming are already here, and my peace and quiet could be interrupted at any moment by cosmic catastrophe . . .

Jesus will return personally

It is this image of Jesus returning as a 'thief in the night' that is really worth considering. Four times the New Testament compares Jesus' return to 'a thief in the night' (Lk. 12:39,40; 1 Thes. 5:2; 2 Pet. 3:10; Rev. 16:15). Such a colourful image points to an element of surprise, but there is more to this image than meets the eye.

More than the thought of suddenness or surprise, it's the idea of being caught unawares when a robber invades your private space, when he rifles through your personal belongings, when he leaves you feeling insecure and afraid. I was speaking last week to a member of my church whose house had just been broken into. What struck me was that she was not concerned about the monetary value of the things that had been taken by the thieves. There was nothing that she could not replace or claim insurance on. But she was much more perturbed that someone had been in her private home. Her 'safe place' was no longer safe. Her personal affairs had been disturbed as drawers lay opened and photograph frames of family smashed.

You see it is not just that Jesus will come at a time when few people are expecting him, but that his return will be very personal. That is surely one of the feelings the New Testament wants to give us through this image of a 'thief in the night'. Jesus will be coming to rifle through the private things in your life and mine that we thought no one else knew about or would ever discover. His coming will bring with it a personal examination, an uncovering of inner motives, our deepest heart desires, our darkest ambitions. That is the feeling that a woman has when she returns home to discover there has been a break-in. The invasion of privacy is more unsettling in many ways than the unexpected timing of the visit.

An invasion of privacy

The coming again will ultimately be an invasion of privacy. Jesus will expose our hearts for what they truly are. Evil will be exposed for what it truly is – not just the outrageous public evil of a Hitler or a Stalin, but the socially acceptable private evil of an amoral lifestyle being lived out without any thought or fear of the Lord.

But this invasion of privacy will not just be for the world. It will begin with the church. God will judge his own people, as Peter himself declares

> it is time for judgment to begin with the family of God (1 Pet. 4:17).

Just imagine the moment when we are at last caught up into the presence of Christ, and are presented in front of his judgement seat at the end of time. Many Christians appear to be unaware that they will face a judgement seat on the last day. They think to themselves, 'Has Christ not dealt with every area of judgement in my life? Do I not have a free ticket to heaven on account of the cross?'

Yes, of course you do. Not that the ticket is really free. It cost Jesus untold agony, and separation from his Father during three hours of intense darkness. It cost him the immeasurable anguish of being perfect, yet being presented to the Father as everything that is vile and deplorable. An eternity's weight of sin – of murder, rape, lies, hatred, gossip, slander, adultery – placed to Jesus' account under the angry eyes of God (2 Cor. 5:21). What a beaten, broken, slandered, bloodied, beautiful, humble, courageous, incomparable, world-winning, eternity-swinging Saviour. But yes, you and I have a 'free' ticket.

This is the beauty of the gospel, and the wonder of God's grace to us. That beautiful word 'atonement' means that Jesus has perfectly and fully 'covered' our sins in the eyes of God. We will never have to answer for our rebellion.

What we need to realize is that the Scriptures refer to two different judgement seats. One is the 'Great White Throne', mentioned in Revelation 20. The issue at the Great White Throne will be the eternal salvation of men and women. This awesome chapter depicts the opening of the 'Book of Life'. The Book of Life contains the names of all those who have been saved by the blood of Christ. As the Book of Life is opened in front of a vast multitude at the end of time, judgement is pronounced

> If anyone's name was not found written in the Book of Life, he was thrown into the Lake of Fire (Rev. 20:15)

However awesome and stark the Great White Throne and the lake of fire might be, no true believers will find themselves there. Our hell is paid for. Or to put it another way, Christ has entered the fire of God's wrath for us. At the cross he fully tasted the Lake of Fire on our behalf, as our sacred substitute, so we cannot be touched by it.

The 'Judgement Seat of Christ'

But, there is another place of judgement that the New Testament describes. Paul refers to the 'Judgement Seat of Christ'. In 2 Corinthians 5, Paul is clearly talking to Christians. He is encouraging them that their earthly bodies are just temporary dwellings, like a tent. One day, when they die, their spirits will leave their tents and be caught up to be with Christ. What a moment of joy that

Jesus is Coming Again

will be for the Christian. But he ends that thought with a more sombre one.

> For we must all appear before the judgment seat of Christ, that each one may receive what is due to him for the things done while in the body, whether good or bad (2 Cor. 5:10).

The issue at the Judgement Seat of Christ will not be the eternal salvation of our souls. But God wants to know what we have made of the lives he has given us; of the grace he has poured out on us; of the gifts he has planted within us. The bar is raised at the Judgement Seat of Christ. As Christians we are such privileged people. We have been let in on the meaning of life, which remains such a mystery to the majority of our planet.

We have been given the gift of the Holy Spirit, who comes alongside us to promote the character of Jesus in our personalities (Rom. 8:1-17). We have been entrusted with the gospel (1 Cor. 4:1). We have been brought into the international family of God who, for all their imperfections, share the same hope we share, and spur us on 'towards love and good deeds' (Heb. 10:24).

To put it crudely, God is looking for a good return on his investment. If we have dribbled away our lives in pointless, apathetic living, he won't keep us out of heaven (my ticket to heaven depends on Jesus' merits, not mine), but he will feel it and we will feel it at the Judgement Seat.

Paul uses a compelling image to describe how our lives will be judged at the Judgement Seat of Christ.

> The fire will test the quality of each man's work (1 Cor. 3:13).

Just as fire tests the purity and value of a metal, so God's fire will test the purity and value of our lives. Fire is searching. It is burning. It uncovers and reveals the true character of the metal. The Judgement Seat of Christ will be the 'moment of truth' for us. The most rigorous examination of our motives. The most intricate testing of our life's work. The most exacting measurement of our zeal.

This kind of rigorous testing is happening already of course. Jesus' fiery eyes are pointed at every church, every gathering of God's people, every believing heart. The letters to the seven churches in Revelation 2 and 3 are really God's assessment of his people. Jesus is the one with the piercing eyes at the end of Revelation 1, who walks among the 'lampstands' (a metaphor for the churches) and judges the value of each church's ministry. The Judgement Seat of Christ will simply be the final accounting of the testing Jesus has been conducting throughout our lives.

The joy of the Judgement Seat

But we are not to imagine that this Judgement Seat will be a joyless event. It all depends on the quality of lives we present at his throne. For burning-heart believers, the Judgement Seat of Christ will be a homecoming. It will be the greatest joy of their lives to hear the words from the Master

> Well done, good and faithful servant! (Mt. 25:21)

When the Master says, 'Well done!' as I stand before him, my heaven will be two heavens. It will be joyous not just because I have passed the divine test of the all-knowing God. It will be wonderful because Jesus himself will mean everything to me on that day, as I stand in my glorified mind and body. I will have a perfect understanding of him. I will appreciate his beauty and wonder and sacrifice like never before. And, I get the sense that when his fire is placed on the quality of my life's work, I will be just desperate to bring a smile to his face.

I will see the nail prints in his hands. I will feel the warmth of his eyes on my soul. I will experience the full radiance of his person.

To know on that 'day of truth' that my life brings pleasure to him, that he feels I have run the race well and been worthy to carry his name, I tell you, there will be no greater sense of elation in the universe.

The loss at the Judgement Seat

But what if we've lived half a life? What if we've been so caught up with our careers, our hobbies, our holidays, even our husbands or wives, that Jesus has only got second best? What will the Judgement Seat be like then – when we realize, in the face of absolute truth and piercing honesty that the total product of our lives is worth no more that the dust that falls from a carpenter's table?

That's the image Paul gives of wasted Christian lives. The works of burning-heart believers produce 'gold and silver and precious stones' when they are exposed to the fire of God's testing. There's something durable, precious and even sparkling about the works of godly men and women. But the wasted lives of compromised Christians who were more interested in their bank accounts, their soccer teams, their satellite TV systems, their homes or gardens than they are in being disciples of Jesus, is likened to 'wood, hay or straw' (1 Cor. 3:12).

The Judgement Seat of Christ will not reveal the hidden sin in the hearts of Christians. Sin is dealt with. The blushing at the throne will not be because God will display some kind of 'video nasty' of our most carnal moments to a watching church who cannot believe their eyes. God is not vindictive that way. But the Judgement Seat will reveal waste, ungratefulness, shallowness, pure laziness. 'I would rather you were hot or cold,' said Jesus to the Christians in Laodicea. 'But you're lukewarm. You're no use to anyone.' (See Rev. 3:16)

There will be no tears in heaven (Rev. 21:4), but there will be a sense of loss in the hearts of believers who know they have been given so very much, and have made so very little of it. God's mercy will cover our sins, but it won't remove our sense of 'loss', if we know deep down we have not lived in a manner of the Christ who hung on a cross for us.

> If it is burned up, he will suffer loss; he himself will be saved, but only as one escaping through the flames (1 Cor. 3:15).

11

Get Ready to Meet Jesus

So, you might ask, if the return of Christ will involve such a thorough examination of our lives, if I will stand in front of a judgement seat, how can I have a heart that burns for his return? How can I look forward to the second coming with longing, if it will lead to such a searching examination of my life? Should I not be afraid of his return? This is where the 'rubber hits the road' in our lives. The way I feel about Jesus' return might actually be a litmus test of the quality of my Christian life. Let me use an illustration. Imagine two students studying Shakespeare in preparation for important exams.

One of them is a brilliant student who has applied himself without compromise to his studies. He does not dread exam day. In fact there is a sense of completion about the exam. An expectant readiness for whatever question will come up. Perhaps he won't get every question right, but he has really fought to get to grips with Shakespeare – so much so that he has moved from being someone who is simply fulfilling course requirements, to being an avid learner who has a genuine passion for Shakespeare's unique writing talents. Shakespeare is almost part of his personality now. The exam will allow him to pour out on paper his love for Shakespeare's artistry, his comic genius, his intricate character development. In fact if there wasn't an exam on Shakespeare he would feel cheated. There would be a sense of deflation.

It's the wayward student who is biting his nails when the alarm rings for exam day. He's been going out every night in the months leading up to the exam. He has an eerie feeling in the pit of his stomach, a sense of unease about his 'day of reckoning'. His whole motivation is to 'scrape through.' He has never loved Shakespeare. Every class is drudgery (the ones he attends at least).

He looks at the minimum 'pass' grade as the promised land. Shakespeare for him is a means to an end, an uncomfortable interruption to his social life and partying. He knows deep down that his studies have just been a sideshow to the other passions that drive his life. It's not that he doesn't realize how important the exams are. It's that he has pushed their importance to the back of his mind in favour of easier pursuits that he loves. He doesn't really understand how anyone can be passionate about Shakespeare.

When he opens the exam paper, he is a stranger to the content. He is thinking up every way possible that he can avoid showing his ignorance. There are no convictions about his answers as his pen hits the paper. Just the thought of 'I hope this is OK! I hope the examiner can't see through me!'

Meanwhile across the exam room, the Shakespeare lover puts his pen down with a sense of accomplishment. His thought as he leaves the exam room is not 'What grade did I get?' but 'I wish I had longer'. Student number two, if 'student' is a suitable name for him, is just relieved it's all over. He takes out a calculator on the way home to try and work out the percentages in his head – 'Did I hit the 40 per cent pass mark? Did I scrape through?' He'll try and not think about the day the results come out.

The Christ exam

It's not a perfect illustration, but it at least gives you a flavour of how we should be feeling about Christ's return. The more I am living for Christ, the more I will be longing for his return. The more I have devoted myself without compromise to his Kingdom, the more I will be excited about his Judgement Seat. The more I love him, the more I will be just longing to see him with every fibre of my being. He is the love of my life, my favourite person to talk to, my specialist subject to talk about. The more I sense his pleasure on my soul, the more I will be longing for the skies to open. I will have a sense of completion, even euphoria, when he opens my heart before his glorious throne, to see a life that has been laid down in his service. That is burning heart Christianity.

But, if Jesus has been a stranger to me for the best part of my life, if his Kingdom has really been no more than the sideshow to the other passions that drive my heart, then I will have a sense of unease – I *ought* to have a sense of unease about the day I will look into his face. Will it be like looking into the face of my heavenly lover, or the face of a distant stranger? To look upon Jesus on that last day as something other than 'home', other than the fulfilment of my deepest longings, would be to discover that we had lived our lives chasing after straw, when gold was within our grasp. The Judgement Seat of Christ will separate the true Christ lovers, from those who have just scraped into paradise.

We can learn a lot from the way Paul looks at the coming again of Christ. In 2 Timothy, the rugged apostle is coming towards the end of his life. He's writing from a prison cell, the kind of scenario he has got used to over years of missionary travels and courageous preaching in hostile circumstances. We are not quite sure historically how close this was to the end of Paul's life, but it is clear from his words that he is preparing for the sunset of his days on earth. Meeting Jesus face to face is just around the corner for him.

As he looks at some of the dark bruising round his battle-hardened legs, and winces a couple of times, recalling earlier beatings he had taken for his preaching, he writes these incredible words to Timothy.

> I am already being poured out like a drink offering, and the time has come for my departure. I have fought the good fight, I have finished the race, I have kept the faith. Now there is in store for me the crown of righteousness, which the Lord, the righteous Judge, will award to me on that day – and not only to me, but also to all who have longed for his appearing (2 Tim. 4:6-8).

These are words that I meditate on often because they keep me going when my Christian walk is a real struggle. It's the last line of these emotion packed verses that grabs my heart. Paul talks about longing 'for his appearing'. You couldn't find a stronger description of the burning-heart believer than this. Someone who is just longing for Jesus' appearing.

Longing for his appearing

Paul doesn't look at the return of Christ with the fear of a stranger walking into a president's palace. He thinks of it as a marathon runner's celebration at the end of the race, a boxer's triumph as the last man standing when the bell rings, a winning actor's unbridled joy on Oscar night.

There is a sense in these words of 'Open me up Lord. See how devoted my heart is to you. I am an open book.' Paul sees his whole life as a love gift to God. An all-consuming act of worship. He describes his life as a 'drink offering' which was part of Old Testament worship ceremonies. That's why he's positively euphoric about meeting Jesus. Jesus is the prize.

It's not that Paul will get every question right on his Christ exam. He was a murderer of Christians before he met Christ. There have been deep sins in his life. Even into his days as a true believer, he was prone to an overbearing personality, which we see when he has a sharp disagreement with Barnabas over the inclusion of Mark on a missionary journey. I certainly would not have wanted to be on the wrong side of an argument with the fiery apostle.

But from the moment a blinding light stopped his tracks on the road to Damascus, Paul's heart has blazed for his Lord. No, he hasn't got everything right, but Jesus is in his bloodstream. The courage of Jesus staggering up a hill carrying his cross has so captivated Paul that he will undergo lashings and public beatings to make sure the name of Jesus is heard in city streets across Asia and Europe.

His heart has burned for every believer in every church he has planted. Part of the pain in his journey has been 'the pressure of my concern for all the churches' (2 Cor. 11:28).

He looks beyond any personal hurts to long for these people he has devoted his life to, to become like Jesus. Even when some Christian preachers who are jealous of him, make trouble for him, and are preaching Jesus out of false motives, he is just delighted that Jesus is being preached (Phil. 1:15-18).

He has fought a good fight. He has chosen not to live a closeted Christian life, hanging on grimly until Christ's return, hoping no one notices him. He has been a troublemaker for Jesus everywhere he has gone. As one vicar lamented about his passionless life

> Everywhere Paul went there was a riot or revival.
> Everywhere I go they serve tea!

Paul has not just fought with flesh and blood human beings, he has wrestled with principalities and powers. That was demonstrated most powerfully when some fake prophets in Ephesus attempt to copy Paul and exorcise demons in Jesus' name. They are shocked to hear the demons speak to them

> Jesus I know, and I know about Paul, but who are you? (Acts 19:15)

Paul had fought such a good fight and run such a good race that his name was known among the demons of hell. The demons did not run away from fake Jewish exorcists who wanted to make a name for themselves – in fact they left the imposters with a fearful beating. The demons fled in front of a man whose life was being poured out on an altar of sacrifice to Christ. Burning-heart believers are dangerous believers. Is your name known in hell? Do the demons tremble?

'There is now in store for me...'

It's because of this life fully spent in Christ's service that Paul is longing for Jesus' appearing. Paul's heart has burnt for God's glory. It has burnt for Christ to be formed in the lives of other believers. His heart has been set ablaze to share the gospel by all means possible to whoever would hear it, Jew or Gentile, whether it meant beatings and ostracism, imprisonment or shipwreck.

And now his heart cannot stop beating for Christ's appearing. He has lived all his days as a pilgrim, totally out of place in this fading world, with his eyes fixed on the unseen, more permanent world of heaven. His prize is not a meagre company pension – what's the point of living for that?

His reward is the 'crown of righteousness' that the Lord will give him on that final day. Paul is thinking here of the wreaths that were handed out to champion athletes at the Greek games in front of a roaring crowd. Paul has expended all the energy of an athlete in his Christian race. He has shown all the discipline of a man who beats his body and makes it his slave (cf. 1 Cor. 9). He disciplines his mind so that the word of Christ 'dwells in him richly' (see Col. 3:16). He disciplines his tongue so that he only says what will 'benefit those who listen', as he teaches, rebukes, corrects and trains them in righteousness.

The crown God will give will not fade like the garlands that drape around the necks of athletes. His crown will last forever. Jesus' appearing will just be joy for Paul. That is why he longs for Jesus' appearing. And that is why we should long for it too.

What's in store for you?

So how are you feeling about Jesus' return? If he were to come tonight like a thief, and catch you living the way you are living, would you be ready for him? Are you longing for him to come? When the first Christians met together, they used to close their meetings with a single word – *maranatha*. That's the word Paul uses at the end of his first letter to the church in Corinth

> Come, O Lord! (1 Cor. 16:22)

Maranatha describes the longing of every burning-heart Christian – 'Come, O Lord!' Come and rescue me from this fallen world. I'm sick of breathing the same air as a world living in rebellion to the rule of God. I long to live under your gracious, generous, consistent, holy leadership. Come and clothe me with Christ. I'm sick of living in this sinful body; this sinful mind that so often disappoints you. As the parched desert longs to be saturated with refreshing rain, I long to see you Lord Jesus, and worship you from the depths of a perfected spirit that will enjoy all your beauty and wonder. I long to grasp the full joy of my salvation that my carnal heart just cannot appreciate this side of glory. *Maranatha*, come quickly, Lord.

Is that how you are feeling about the return of Christ? Are you truly longing for his appearing? It is only Christ-intoxicated hearts who will fully revel in all that heaven has to offer. Some Christians I know are longing for the new bodies that heaven will bring them. For the day when every tear will be wiped away, the old will go and the new will come.

But that's not the question we're asking here. We're asking 'Are you longing for *his* appearing? Longing for heaven and longing for Jesus' return isn't necessarily the same thing. If we imagine heaven to be some kind of perfect playground in the sky where all our deepest dreams come true, even the most wasteful Christian will get excited about that. The question is, 'What are your deepest dreams?'

Heaven won't be heaven because the streets are paved with gold, or because we have a mansion with our name on it. Heaven will be heaven because God is there. The crescendo of heaven comes with the announcement

> Now the dwelling of God is with men, and he will live with them. They will be his people, and God himself will be their God (Rev. 21:3).

Heaven will be heaven because Christ will be enthroned. He will be heaven's focus, the centre of attention, the theme of the angelic choirs.

> I did not see a temple in the city, because the Lord God Almighty and the Lamb are its temple. . . . the glory of God gives it light, and the Lamb is its lamp (Rev. 21:22,23).

Is that what you are living for and longing for with your whole heart? Seeing him, being with him, being like him, being caught up with him forever and ever and ever?

Heaven was built by Christ for those who love him with burning hearts. Jesus' own description of his glorious return to his beloved disciples in the upper room is marked by its understated simplicity

if I go and prepare a place for you, I will come back
and take you to be with me where I am (Jn. 14:3).

Forget the fanfare, forget the rolling back of the clouds, forget the multitudes of redeemed singing in a magnificent assembly, forget the crowns, forget the wiping away of tears, forget the sapphires and emeralds, the new bodies, the eternal state. This is what heaven is about. Christ longs to be with his loved ones. He longs to be united to the people for whom he shed his blood. Do we long to be with him? Is your heart 'longing for his appearing'? Those who will feel most at home in heaven are Christ-lovers.

So what if I'm not longing to meet him?

Perhaps as you read this you are thinking to yourself, 'I really wish my deepest desire was to see Christ. I so much want him to be the "first love" of my life (Rev. 2:4), and yet if I'm absolutely honest, there are other things that excite me more. What can I do about this? I cannot just conjure up feelings like that.'

The character of Peter is always so encouraging when we discover that our devotion to Christ is something less than it ought to be. There was no doubting Peter's sincerity in his last walk with Jesus on that beach. 'Lord, you know all things; you know that I love you' (Jn. 21:17) was not a throwaway line from Peter to get Jesus off his back. He genuinely did love Christ.

But his love was not the finished article yet. If it had been, he clearly would not have denied his Lord so vehemently with oaths and curses in the courtyard of the High Priest just a few days earlier. Peter clearly needed a fresh infusion of the Holy Spirit on the Day of Pentecost (Acts 2) before his devotion to Christ would lead to uncompromising preaching in dangerous circumstances.

And that is, I suppose, where we all are at the end of the day. Somewhere on that continuum between a fragile and full throttle love for Christ – needing a fresh infusion of the Holy Spirit. God knows full well that our love for Christ is something that needs to flower over time, like a marriage that matures with the passing of the years. What God is looking for is that we are moving in the right direction. That, like Peter, we regularly want to go on walks with the Lord. That we don't run away when he wants to challenge us about our frail devotion.

If you are anxious about the strength of your love for Christ, it is a clear sign that you have godly desires. It is the work of the Holy Spirit in our hearts to make us anxious in that way – if we weren't anxious we would have no desire to change. Anxiety over our devotion to Christ is actually a sign of healthy spiritual life within us. Be honest with Jesus about your fragile love, about the fact that you don't long for his appearing as much as you ought, and ask him passionately for a heart to love him more. I can't think of a prayer that would be more pleasing to the Lord. And gradually, as each day passes, and you continue in all your fragile ups and downs to walk with him, you will start to long just a little bit more, for the day you will walk with him in glory (Rev. 7:17).

Christ and the church

Ultimately Christianity is about Christ. History is 'his story'. You and I as Christians are being prepared as a gift from God the Father to God the Son (see Jesus' intimate prayer for his disciples in John 17:6-10). We are a bride being prepared for a bridegroom. When Paul is giving instructions to husbands and wives, he says in effect that human beings were given marriage as an illustration of a much more profound mystery. Human marriage illustrates beautifully the relationship between Christ and the church that God has planned from eternity

> 'For this reason a man will leave his father and mother and be united to his wife, and the two will become one flesh.' This is a profound mystery – but I am talking about Christ and the church (Eph. 5:31,32).

What stunning words these are. Jesus has left his Father in heaven to become united to his bride the church – that's you and me. When he comes again he is coming for his bride. Heaven will begin with a marriage between Christ and the church. Think of all the intimacy, the joy, the faithfulness and commitment, the inner longings of the marriage relationship. That is what burning-heart Christians share with Christ.

This is the whole point of life, the point of the cross, the purpose of your salvation. You were saved for Jesus. You belong to him. And ultimately, the story of our lives here on earth is the story of finding our lover, getting to know our lover, serving our lover, until the day we see him face to face in unhindered communion.

Is Jesus your reason for living?

This is what the burning heart boils down to. When you look at your own heart today, can you honestly say, 'Jesus is my reason for living'? There are too many Christians who are living half-hearted lives. Too many who are going through the motions of their religion. They sit in church but never really enter God's presence. They sing songs, but not with hearts aflame. They read the Bible but haven't fallen in love with its author. They break bread and drink wine more out of routine than thankfulness. They've signed a doctrinal statement, but haven't signed their life away to him.

Let me urge you, don't reach heaven as someone who has just managed to escape the flames. Don't stumble over the finish line wishing you could spend a few more days in this broken, desolate world. Don't look into Jesus' eyes on that last day with an aching feeling in your heart – 'I wish I had given him more.'

We only have one life to live. We have such a short time to live it. Jesus is our reason for living. Make him your delight. Serve him, obey him, speak about him, worship him, teach your family to honour him, read about him, talk to him, make music in your heart to him, question him, study him, laugh with him, cry with him, share your best moments with him. Find in him the secret of the burning heart.

Review

- Our hearts need to burn for the return of Christ. His literal future return to earth is as fundamental to our faith as the cross and the resurrection. God's story does not make sense without this final consummation.
- Christ's coming will be very personal to every Christian, and will lead to the Judgement Seat of Christ where the quality of our Christian lives will be measured – some will suffer loss for wasted living,

others will be overjoyed as they receive crowns from the Saviour they have loved.
- Like Paul, we should be 'longing for his appearing'. Those who are most inspired by Christ's return, the Judgement Seat and the heaven that awaits, are those who have loved Christ with burning hearts and enjoyed intimate communion with him. They are truly ready for the Master's return.
- The story of the Bible is the story of God looking for a bride for his Son. We should long to be with Christ as much as he longs to be with us.

For personal study

- The author claims that 'the return of Christ is as fundamental to Christianity as the cross and the resurrection'. Why is Christ's second coming such an important doctrine?
- What aspects of your life do you feel will matter most to Christ when you stand before him? What steps can you take to honour him more in these areas?
- We are a bride being prepared for our heavenly bridegroom – how does this thought impact:
  - Your devotional life (praise, prayer, Bible study)
  - Your public witness
  - Your attitude to suffering
  - Your attitude towards Christ's return

Reflect on the book as a whole:

- What biblical truth has most challenged you?
- What pursuits do you need to give more time to?
- What relationships do you need to work on?
- What attitudes do you need to change?

Epilogue

> Were not our hearts burning within us while he talked with us on the road and opened the Scriptures to us? (Lk. 24:32)

Where do we go from here?

You might be thinking by now, 'This all sounds great, but what do I do about it?' We said at the beginning that this book is not about discovering some spiritual experience that turns every cloudy moment in our lives into a golden sunset. God does not want us to be spiritual sunbathers just lying around waiting to be 'zapped' from heaven.

Of course, there are unique spiritual moments in our lives when we are full of the joy of the Holy Spirit, and almost feel like we can touch heaven. These show us God's sovereign grace in our lives. Jesus himself had powerful moments of rich spiritual experience with heaven (Lk. 10:21). But it is difficult to read the Bible and come to the conclusion that true Christian discipleship has no struggle. Quite the reverse in fact.

Paul tells Timothy in effect to be deadly serious about his faith, to get into God's gym and 'train for godliness'. The burning heart is not some instant fix. Developing a passion for God's glory, a longing love for God's people, a courageous witness to God's world, and a holy longing for Christ's return has effort and struggle written all over it.

Paul tells Timothy in 2 Timothy 2:3-7 (a great burning-heart passage) that his training for godliness involved becoming like a 'good soldier' who 'endures hardship', like an athlete competing for a prize, even like a 'hard-working farmer', with all the rigour and lack of razzamatazz attached to such an image. There are no shortcuts to the burning heart – there never have been. But there is real grace to meet us along the way. Ultimately the burning heart is given by God to those who are striving to live their lives according to God's passions.

Paul puts it beautifully when he sums up all his work for God

> To this end I labour, struggling with all his energy, which so powerfully works in me (Col. 1:29).

The burning heart comes through 'labour', and 'struggling' hand in hand with God's 'energy'. God energizes and 'powerfully works' through the dedicated disciple who is striving to think and feel and act and will with God in a world that hates its Maker.

Sweating in God's gym

To have a heart that burns for God's glory without the disciplined, thoughtful, sometimes disturbing study of

God's Word every day, is a nonsense. To love God's people as God does, without having to absorb serious hurt, or sacrificing yourself at inconvenient times to serve others, is naïve. To witness for Christ to work colleagues and family members without feeling the sting of rejection, the anguish of seeing people we are praying for constantly rebut our approaches, is unheard of. To be ready for Christ's return without battling against the temptations this colourful, seditious world has to offer, is a complete contradiction.

God gives us his energy as we strive, like athletes sweating in God's gym. He works powerfully through us in our struggle. A burning heart is an enduring heart, a persevering heart. It's a heart that sees pain as God's anvil to shape us, disappointment as the inevitable outcome of representing the 'Man of Sorrows', persecution as sharing in Christ's sufferings. A burning heart is often a broken heart.

> The sacrifices of God are a broken spirit; a broken and a contrite heart, O God, you will not despise (Ps. 51:17).

But it is in our brokenness that we are remade. If God is to take our hearts as they are – full of sin, apathetic, in love with a shallow world – and turn them into hearts that burn for him, the process will cost us. We need to allow his divine chisel to smash away at us, until we become his 'work of art' (Eph. 2:10).

Are you ready for the struggle? The struggle starts on your knees. It starts by telling God who you want to be for him. Acknowledging to him that you cannot get there without the energy of his Holy Spirit. It starts by opening his Word with a fresh desire to understand and long for his glory. God's glory is the uncluttered motivation of the burning heart. If we are striving for anything other than his glory, then God's energy will not come to meet us, because we are working at cross purposes to God.

Begin by learning how to love God's glory, how to want what he wants, and the energy and power of the Spirit will meet you there. I don't write this as the master trying to teach the pupil what he has discovered. I wish I desired God's glory in everything, more than I do. But I have experienced something of the burning heart during times when his glory has become my focus. I have also experienced a parched heart, when my own pleasures become my God.

Give me the burning heart every time.

Lord, revive your chosen people,
Break the chains of apathy,
Stir our hearts again to tremble,
At the feet of deity,
We have lost our sense of wonder,
King Immortal, Sovereign Friend,
Come revive your Name among us,
Give us burning hearts again!

Let me see the King of Glory,
Take the scales from my eyes,
Dressed in sovereign power and splendour,
Holy monarch of the skies,
Take me to your holy temple,
Where the angels spread their wings,
Let my heart be captivated,
By the glory of the King!

Epilogue

Lord, arouse your chosen people,
As you did in ancient days,
Moses glowing in your presence,
As you took your veil away,
Jesus shining on the mountain,
'This is my beloved Son',
Stir our hearts and minds to worship,
El Shaddai, the Holy One.

(J.M., 2005)

The Bible Doctrine of Man. PETERBOROUGH
EPWORTH EXPRESS 1951